A
RICHARD WAGNER
DICTIONARY

By EDWARD M. TERRY

GREENWOOD PRESS, PUBLISHERS
WESTPORT, CONNECTICUT

Originally published in 1939
by The H. W. Wilson Company, New York

Reprinted from an original copy in the collections
of the Brooklyn Public Library

First Greenwood Reprinting 1971

Library of Congress Catalogue Card Number 79-109865

SBN 8371-4356-X

Printed in the United States of America

PREFACE

This book is a result of the writer's experience in trying to learn something of Richard Wagner, the great poet-composer, and his works. Reading the usual run of books on the subject one comes across many casual allusions to people, places and other particulars which presuppose a certain knowledge on one's part that can be acquired only by broad reading or by delving deeply into the mass of material out of which the books are made.

It is with a view to providing a convenient volume of reference for the general reader that this dictionary has been compiled, thus promoting his understanding and appreciation of what he is trying to read or study.

Included, in the appendix, is a bibliography of some of the better-known books dealing with Wagner and various phases of his work, which it is hoped may be helpful, not only to the student but to the less-concerned reader as well.

The so-called Leading Motives of the music-dramas may also be found in the appendix, arranged under the proper headings for ready reference. It is well understood, of course, that the names or titles of the motives are purely arbitrary—Wagner himself having no disposition to designate them by name—but follow for the most part the common designations which have been given to them by various writers.

Wagner's Prose Works come in for considerable attention owing to their importance in gaining a thorough knowledge of the music revolutionist that he was and of his ideas.

Occasion has been taken in many instances to gather fresh facts in order to fill out adequately items which, because of lapse of time or otherwise, other books have failed to cover.

Grateful acknowledgment of assistance is due to, among others: Städtisches Verkehrsamt, Bayreuth; Messrs. Breitkopf & Härtel, Leipzig; The Metropolitan Opera Association, Inc., New York; Dr. E. Klöti, Herrn Stadtpräsidente (Mayor) of Zürich, Switzerland, *and* my wife.

E. M. TERRY

East Orange, New Jersey
September, 1939

CONTENTS

NOTE. The letters P.W. (Prose Works), followed by a figure, in the text refer to the so-designated volume in William Ashton Ellis's translation of *Gesammelte Schriften,* issued in eight volumes by Kegan Paul, Trench, Trubner & Co., London, 1892-99.

"My aim was to prove the possibility of an art-form in which the highest and deepest things that the human intellect can grasp should be presented in such a way as to be intelligible to the simple receptive faculty derived from purely human sympathy, and in such a definite and convincing form that critical reflection should be altogether unnecessary for its comprehension."

RICHARD WAGNER, PROSE WORKS,
Vol. vii,118.

A
RICHARD WAGNER
DICTIONARY

Actors and Singers. P.W. 5. Written shortly after the laying of the foundation-stone of the Bayreuth Festspielhaus, May 22, 1872. Published in that year by Fritzch of Leipzig.

Adriano. A character in *Rienzi*; mezzo-soprano. Son of Steffano Colonna. Act 1, Nos. 1, 2, 3; Act 2, Nos. 6, 7; Act 3, Nos. 9, 10; Act 4, Nos. 11, 12; Act 5, Nos. 15, 16. Rôle created by Schröder-Devrient.

Agoult, Countess d'. Born Marie de Flavigny at Frankfort-on-the-Main about 1800. Married Count d'Agoult 1827. Died 1876. A French authoress, known as "Daniel Stern." Companion of Franz Liszt and the mother of his three children, all of whom he legitimized. Liszt parted from the Countess in the middle of the year 1844.

Alberich. A character in *The Ring;* baritone-bass. Chief of the Nibelungs; a hairy and uncouth gnome.
>   *Das Rheingold*, Scenes 1, 3, 4. Rôle created by Fischer.
>   *Siegfried*, Act 2. Rôle created by Carl Hill.
>   *Götterdämmerung*, Act 2. Rôle created by Carl Hill.

Albumblatt, for Frau Betty Schott, in E ♭. Listed in Musical Works. Written Jan. 1, 1875. Published 1876 or 1877.

Albumblatt, for Fürstin Metternich, in C, Ein. Listed in Musical Works. Written 1861. Published 1871.

Album-Sonata, for Frau Mathilde Wesendonck, in E ♭. Listed in Musical Works. Written 1853. (Album-leaf "Arrival at the Black Swans," for Countess Pourtalès, in A ♭. Published 1877).

Ali. A character in *The Saracen Woman*; bass.

Allegro to the aria of Aubrey in the "Vampire," by Marschner. Listed in Musical Works. In F minor. Score, 142 bars of additional text and music, instead of the 58 bars of the original, dated Würzburg, Sept. 23, 1833, in possession of Herr W. Tappert, Berlin.

Am stillen Herd. Walther's air in *Die Meistersinger*. Act 1.

> By silent hearth in winter-tide,
> When house and hall in snow did hide,
> How once the Spring so sweetly smiled
> And soon should wake to glory mild,
> An ancient book my sire compiled
> Set all before me duly:
> Sir Walter von der Vogelweid
> Has been my master truly.

Amfortas. A character in *Parsifal*; baritone-bass. Son of Titurel, ruler of the kingdom of the Grail. Acts 1, 3. Rôle created by Theodor Reichmann.

Ananda. The hero of a drama entitled *The Victors*, of which Wagner made a sketch bearing date of May 16, 1856.

Angel, The. Listed in Musical Works. The first of five songs under the general title "Five Poems." Composed in 1862. English by Francis Hueffer.

Anwendung der Musik auf das Drama, Über die. See Application of Music to the Drama, On the.

Apel, Theodor. (1811-1867) Student at St. Nicholas School, Leipzig, with Wagner. Traveled with him to Bohemia. He lived as a gentleman of means. He suffered from an accident early in life, having fallen off a horse. He wrote a great deal. From 1838 he was totally blind.

Application of Music to the Drama, On the. P.W. 6. Published in the *Bayreuther Blätter* Nov. 1879.

Arrangements (Musical). See Musical Works.

Art and Climate. P.W. 1. Written in Zürich 1850; printed in the Stuttgart *Deutsche Monatsschrift* April 1850. Treats of the influence of climate upon man's capacity for Art.

Art and Revolution. P.W. 1. With Introduction. Written in Paris during the Saxony revolutionary period of 1848-49 and published in 1849. Used as the Preface to Vols. III and IV of his collected writings (*Gesammelte Schriften*) for the edition of 1872. The Introduction was written at Triebschen July 1871, and applies to Art and Revolution, The Art-Work of the Future, Opera and Drama, etc. It develops contrasts and differences between Greek and modern art.

Artist and Critic. P.W. 8. Written in 1846; published in the *Dresdener Anzeiger* August 14, 1846.

Artist and Publicity, The. P.W. 7. See German Musician in Paris, A. Article No. 6.

Arts of Poetry and Tone in the Drama of the Future, The. P.W. 2. See Opera and Drama, Part 3.

Art-Work of the Future, The. P.W. 1. Written in Zürich 1849 and published by Wigand of Leipzig in that year. General heads are:

1. Man and Art, in General.

11

2. Artistic Man and Art as derived directly from him.
3. Man Shaping Art from Nature's Stuffs.
4. Outlines of the Art-Work of the Future.
5. The Artist of the Future.

Asyl. "Refuge," or "Haven of Rest." Name bestowed on Wagner's little house near the Wesendoncks at Enge, Switzerland. Rented from Mr. Wesendonck for a small sum. Wagner lived there from April, 1857, to August, 1858.

At Weber's Grave. Listed in Musical Works.
(a) Funeral march for wind instruments on motives from *Euryanthe*;
(b) Double quartet for voices.
Performed Dec. 15, 1844. Score of (b) published 1872.

L'Attente. See Waiting.

Auber, Reminiscences of. P.W. 5. Published in *Musikalisches Wochenblatt*, Nov. 1871.

Aufführung des Tannhäuser, Über die. See Performing of Tannhäuser, On the.

August 25, 1870. See Poems.

Author's Introduction to Vol. II of the "Gesammelte Schriften." P.W. 7. Written in 1871 at Triebschen.

Autobiographic Sketch. P.W. 1. His life down to 1842, prepared at the request of his friend Heinrich Laube, for publication 1843 in the *Zeitung für die Elegante Welt*.

B

Bacchanal. The musical themes associated with the Bacchanalian revels in Tannhaüser, in the domain of Venus.

Baroncello. A character in *Rienzi*; tenor. A Roman citizen. Act 1, No. 1; Act 2, No. 7; Act 3, No. 8; Act 4, No. 11; Act 5, No. 16. Rôle created by Reinhold.

Bathilde. A character in *Wieland the Smith*. Daughter of Neiding, the King of the Niaren.

Baudelaire, Charles. Friend and visitor of Wagner in Paris.

Baumgartner, Wilhelm. A music teacher in Zürich; friend of Wagner and dubbed by him "Boom." Born May 5, 1820; died 1867. See *Neue Musik-Zeitung*, Stuttgart, May 20, 1920, p.250.

Bayreuth. A city in Bavaria, Germany, in 1891 of about 20,000 inhabitants, now (1938) 40,000. On the Red Main. Mentioned in documents of the 12th century. It is the district town and headquarters of the Bavarian Ostmark. The built-up area comprises 2,050 acres; total area 5,375 acres. Height above sea-level 1,115 feet. It is about three hours by rail from Nuremberg in the northeastern corner of Bavaria. The name signifies a *rod* or *reuth* (a clearing), a place wrung from the wilderness and given over to culture.

Here a special theatre was built at the instigation of King Ludwig II for the *Nibelung* dramas. (See Festspielhaus. Also J. P. Jackson's *The Bayreuth of Wagner*.)

Wagner first visited Bayreuth in 1871. He thought he could use the old Royal Opera-House, built by Margrave Frederick in 1748, for performances of *The Ring*. Charmed by the beautiful surroundings of the city he declared, "Here is the site for the Nibelung Theatre." He selected Bayreuth because it made a very agreeable impression upon him; it was off the beaten track of artistic life and the official

13

representatives were willing to meet his wishes and aid in the promotion of his ideas. It gave him two lots for his theatre and for his own house in the suburbs, Wahnfried. He was also influenced in his selection by his obligation to King Ludwig to erect his theatre within the boundaries of Bavaria. Here died and was buried his friend and artistic supporter, Franz Liszt.

Notable points of interest are the castles and parks of Fantasie and the Hermitage. Jean Paul (Jean Paul Friedrich Richter), one of the greatest of German poets and humanists, lived and died at No. 384 Friedrichstrasse. A bronze statue of the poet was presented to the city by King Ludwig I of Bavaria.

THE HERMITAGE

"And now we approach the palace and gardens of the Hermitage, one of the most delightful creations of the margravial period. Here Napoleon spent a night, his sleep disturbed by the famous ghost "die weisse Frau." And here at night the unhappy Ludwig II conversed with Bayreuth's great genius Richard Wagner. The distant Festival Theatre is seen through the trees and Bayreuth's present and future greet its glorious past."

MARGRAVIAL OPERA HOUSE

"The visitor coming from the station has a very pleasant view of the town as he enters the Opernstrasse. On his left is the Opera House, built by St. Pierre, with a graceful curved balcony and graceful pillars and pilasters; the cornice is ornamented with numerous fine statues. The interior, decorated by Bibiena, richly gilded and carved, with a painted ceiling, is of great artistic merit; the stage is of vast dimensions. In this beautiful theatre the court festivals of the margraves took place. Richard Wagner heard of this beautiful theatre which at that time had the largest stage in Germany; and though it could not be adapted to his technical requirements it was decisive in his choice of Bayreuth as the scene of his festival performances. After the laying of the foundation-stone of his Festival Theatre in 1872, he here conducted a fine rendering of Beethoven's Ninth Symphony in the Old Opera House."

14

The New Palace

"Margrave Frederic and Margravine Wilhelmina, the favorite sister of Frederic the Great, to whom Bayreuth owes its architectural development during the baroque and rokoko periods, had the New Palace built by Joseph St. Pierre after the old palace had been destroyed by fire in 1753. The central part contains a large hall which was used for festivals, ornamented on the outside with pillars and figures; plain left and right wings extend in a straight line on either side. The left wing on the Glasenappweg (side entrance) contains the Richard Wagner Memorial Museum."

Richard Wagner Memorial Museum

"Glasenappweg, in the left wing of the New Palace. It has recently been enlarged and consists of 23 rooms arranged in 11 sections. 'Love - tragedy', these were the last words which Richard Wagner wrote shortly before his death. On the 13th February, 1883, his restless and indomitable spirit was occupied with a monograph on the theme 'The womanly side of human nature' when he was suddenly attacked by heart failure. 'Love - tragedy', the great mystery of life, possessed his soul to the end. In a room apart in the Richard Wagner Museum are still preserved some earthly tokens which speak to us so silently but poignantly of the past. Above the small sofa on which he must often have sat in his home at Venice, and on which he died, hangs the death-mask of the master. But from it there seems to descend an almost inearthly radiance as if it would say to us: the master lives eternally in his works. His whole life—struggle and final victory—are here manifest to us in mementoes, pictures and manuscripts, in truth a biography of his life, and we are shown how they are culturally bound up with the master's work extending through the years to our own times. Helena Wallem is the founder and director of the Museum. Authorized by the town of Bayreuth she was able in the course of ten years of unceasing labour to complete this place of remembrance and research aided in her work by the self-sacrificing idealism of such noble patrons as Robert Bartsch of Copenhagen and Heinrich Bales of Cologne."

The above quotations are from a booklet issued by Städtisches Verkehrsamt, *Bayreuth.*

See Bayreuth. P.W. 5.

1. Final Report on the Fates and Circumstances that attended the execution of the stage-festival-play *Der Ring des Nibelungen* down to the founding of Wagner Societies.

2. The Festival-playhouse (Festspielhaus) at Bayreuth, with an account of its foundation-stone. Written in 1873. Addressed to Baroness Marie von Schleinitz, afterward Countess von Wolkenstein-Trostburg. Published by Fritzch in 1873.

Bayreuther Blätter. A monthly periodical founded by Richard Wagner and edited by Baron von Wolzogen as a mode of communicating with the Wagner Societies. First number January 1878. In it first appeared essays written by Wagner during the last six years of his life. Collected in Vol. X of his *Collected Works.*

These publications are in Prose Works, Vol. 6 (Ellis). They bear upon plans connected with his settlement in Bayreuth, together with his shorter "Introduction." Also larger essays of later years which appeared in the same journal.

1. To the Presidents of Wagner Societies (Vereins).
2. Proposed Bayreuth "School."
3. Introduction to First Number of the *Bayreuther Blätter.*
4. Introduction to a work of Hans von Wolzogen's.
5. Postponement of *Parsifal.*
6. Introduction to the year 1880.
7. Announcement of *Parsifal* performance.
8. Introduction to a work of Count Gobineau's.

Beckmesser, Sixtus. One of the mastersingers in *Die Meistersinger*; bass. Town clerk. Acts 1, 2, 3. Rôle created by Hölzel.

A coarse and vulgar pedant.

"Hans Sachs I took as a representation of the art-productive spirit of the Folk, and set him in contrast to the petty-fogging bombast of the other Mastersingers; to whose ridiculous pedantry of *tablatur* and prosody I gave concrete expression in the figure of the 'marker'."

RICHARD WAGNER, *in the original sketch dated Marienbad, July 16, 1845.*

In the third prose sketch of *Die Meistersinger,* written about 1861, when Wagner had met Edward Hanslick, the famous critic and did not like him, the name given to the Marker is Hanslick; later it was changed to Beckmesser. It was Wagner's intention to caricature his hated critic. Knowledge of this on the part of Hanslick, it is thought, had much to do with the critic's attacks upon the composer.

Beethoven. Ludwig von Beethoven, famous composer. Born at Bonn probably Dec. 16, 1770. Died March 26, 1827 (at Vienna?) Greatly admired by Wagner. For references to Beethoven in Wagner's writings see Glasenapp's *Wagner Encyclopädie.* Wagner conducted a Beethoven Festival for his birthday on May 22, 1872, being then 59 years old. The Ninth Symphony was chosen, the place Bayreuth in the old opera house.
See *Beethoven,* P.W. 5. Written in 1870 and published by E. W. Fritzch, Leipzig, 1870.

Beethoven's Choral Symphony. P.W. 7. Written at Dresden, 1846, together with a program. Excerpt from Richard Wagner's *Memoirs,* written between 1866 and 1871.

Beethoven's Heroic Symphony. See Explanatory Programmes, No. 1.

Beethoven's Ninth Symphony. Listed in Musical Works. Arrangement for piano, 1830. Unpublished. See Rendering of Beethoven's Ninth Symphony, The.

Beethoven's Overture to Coriolanus. See Explanatory Programmes, No. 2.

Bellini: A Word in Season. Article by Wagner in the *Riga Zuschauer* Dec. 7 (19), 1837. Reprinted in *Bayreuther Blätter* Dec. 1885, and in Kurschner's *Wagner Jahrbuch*, 1886, p.381. In this article Wagner praised Bellini and vocal melody. P.W. 8. (No. 3 in the list of articles not included in *Gesammelte Schriften.*)

> Vincenzo Bellini, composer. Born at Catania, Sicily, Nov. 1, 1801. Composed the operas *La Sonnambula*, *Norma*, *I Puritani*, etc. Died Sept. 24, 1835.

Bemerkungen zur Aufführung der Oper "Der fliegende Holländer." See Remarks on Performing the Opera *The Flying Dutchman*.

Benewitz, Anna. Daughter of Ernst Benewitz, wife of Emmanuel Wagner. Born 1670, died 1718. Mother of Samuel Wagner, the younger.

Berggeist, Der, oder Die drei Wünsche. See Incidental Music to a Fairy Farce by Gleich. Listed in Musical Works.

Bericht an Seine Majestät den König Ludwig II von Bayern über eine in München zu errichtende deutsche Musikschule. See Music-School for Munich, A.

Bericht über die Aufführung der neunten Symphonie von Beethoven. See Beethoven's Choral Symphony.

Bericht über die Aufführung des "Tannhäuser" in Paris. See Report on the Production of Tannhäuser in Paris, A.

Bericht über eine erste Opernaufführung. Account of a first operatic performance. See Liebesverbot, Das.

Bericht über eine neue Pariser Oper. See Halévy's *Reine de Chypre.*

Berlioz, Hector. Friend and visitor of Wagner in Paris, afterward his enemy. Born at La Côte, St. André, near Grenoble, on Dec. 11, 1803. Died at Paris March 8, 1869. Composer of *The Damnation of Faust.* See Letter to Hector Berlioz, A.

Bertz, Johanna Rosina. The name is also spelt "Berthis." See Wagner, Johanna Rosina.

Bestimmung der Oper, Über die. See Destiny of Opera, The.

Bibliography. This will be found in the appendix, p. 179.

Biebrich. A town on the Rhine, opposite Mayence, where Wagner dwelt while composing the music of *Die Meistersinger.*

Biterolf. A character in *Tannhäuser;* bass. Act 1, scene 4; Act 2, scene 4; Act 3, scene 3. Rôle created by Wächter.

Blanchefleur. In *Tristan,* the wife of Rivalin, King of Parmenia. Sister of Marke in Cornwall.

Börne, Ludwig. Author. Influenced Wagner in his daily life and thought. Celebrated journalist, critic and politician of Jewish extraction. Born at Frankfort-on-the-Main in 1786. He was converted to Christianity. Founded in Paris *Le Balance.* Edited the *Wage* 1818-1821, a periodical for literature, science and art. Died in Paris 1837.

Brangäne. A character in *Tristan and Isolde;* mezzo-soprano. Isolde's attendant. Act 1, scenes 1, 2, 3, 5, 6, 7; Act 2, scenes 1, 2, 3; Act 3, scenes 3, 4. Rôle created by Mlle. Deinet.

19

Braut, Die hohe. A novel by Heinrich König, which led Wagner to prepare a sketch of a five-act opera by that name. He mailed the manuscript to Eugène Scribe, librettist of the *Huguenots*, in Paris, but nothing came of it.

Breitkopf & Härtel. A famous German firm of music publishers in Leipzig, founded in 1719 by Bernhardt Christoph Breitkopf under his name only, becoming B. C. Breitkopf & Son in 1765. It became eventually the first printing house in Germany. Bernhardt's grandson, Christoph Gottlob, disliking the printing business, gave it up and put it in the hands of his friend Gottfried Christoph Härtel, son of Dr. Christoph Härtel, Burgomaster of Schneeberg. He published works of Mozart, Haydn, Bach, and many other composers. He started the *Allgemeine Musikalische Zeitung*, the leading musical periodical. Printed Wagner's piano sonata, Opus 1, and a polonaise in D for four hands, Opus 2.

Bridal Chorus. In *Lohengrin*, Act 3, scene 1. "Faithful and true, we lead ye forth." Expresses the merriment of the wedding festival. The bridal procession of men and women enters the bridal chamber, the ladies leading Elsa and the King and nobles leading Lohengrin, both being preceded by pages.

Brief an H. v. Wolzogen. See End of the Patronat-Verein.

Brief an Hector Berlioz, Ein. See Letter to Hector Berlioz, A.

Brockhaus, Friedrich Arnold. Brother-in-law of Wagner. Born at Dortmund in 1772. German publisher and founder of the firm of Brockhaus at Leipzig.

Brünnhilde. A character in *The Ring*; soprano. Daughter of Wotan; a valkyrie.
Die Walküre, Acts 2, 3. Rôle created by Fräulein Stehle.
Siegfried, Act 3. Rôle created by Amalia Friedrich-Materna.
Götterdämmerung, Prelude, Acts 1, 2, 3. Rôle created by Amalia Friedrich-Materna.

Brünnhilde's War Cry. "Ho-yo-to-ho! Ho-yo-to-ho! Hi-ya-ha! Hi-ya-ha!"
Sung by Brünnhilde at the beginning of Act 2, *Die Walküre*.

Bühnenfestspiel. Stage-festival-play. To be performed in three days and a fore-evening. See Ring of the Nibelungs, The.

Bülow, Hans Guido von. Pianist and conductor, a pupil and son-in-law of Liszt. Born Jan. 8, 1830, at Dresden. Wagner's acquaintance with him began at Zürich and he was a conductor of Wagner's greatest works. Edward Dannreuther called him "the foremost pianist of that most advanced school of pianoforte-playing founded by Chopin and developed by Liszt." He defended the musical ideas of the new school of which Liszt and Wagner were the protagonists. Married 1857 Liszt's daughter Cosima, later the wife of Wagner. Died in Cairo, Egypt, Feb. 12, 1894.

Bulwer-Lytton, Edward. Edward George Earle Lytton, Baron Lytton. Noted British novelist. Born at Heydon Hall, in Norfolk, in 1803. Died Jan. 18, 1873. Author of the novel, *Rienzi, the Last of the Tribunes*, published in 1835, which was used as a basis for the opera of the same name.

Burello. A character in *The Saracen Woman;* bass.

Burrell, Mary. Author of *Richard Wagner, His Life and Works from 1813-1834.* Material collected by Mrs. Burrell is in possession of the Bok family, of Philadelphia. Only one volume was finished, issued in London, 1898, as she died in that year.

C

Capitulation, A. P.W. 5. Written in the winter of 1870-71. Published in Vol. IX of *Gesammelte Schriften.* A parody on the capitulation of France in the Franco-German war. Characters introduced are:
Victor Hugo Mottu (Commander of Battalion),
Perrin (Director of the Opera),
Lefèvre (Diplomat),
Keller and Dollfuss (Alsatians),
Diedenhofer (from Lorraine),
Véfour, Chevet and Vachette. All these are chorus-leaders.
Also: Jules Faure, Jules Ferry, Jules Simon and Gambetta (Members of the Government); Nadar, Flourens, Mégy and Turcos.
Scene is laid in Paris, late autumn, 1870.

Carnevalslied. Listed in Musical Works. See Carnival Song.

Carnival Song. From *Das Liebesverbot,* 1835-36. Reprinted at Brunswick, 1855.

Carvalho, Léon (Carvaille). Friend and visitor of Wagner in Paris. Born Jan. 18, 1825 in Port Louis, Ile de France; died in Paris Dec. 29, 1897. Educated at the Paris Conservatoire. A stage singer early in his career, later French impressario. From 1856 to 1869, except 1861, director of the Théâtre Lyrique, afterward at the Vaudeville; 1874-75 stage manager at the Paris Opéra; 1876 director of the Opéra Comique. Following a disastrous fire in 1887 he was fined and for a time was imprisoned, but in 1891 was acquitted and reinstated.

Cecco del Vecchio. A character in *Rienzi*; bass. A Roman citizen. Act 1, No. 1; Act 2, No. 7; Act 3, No. 8; Act 4, No. 11; Act 5, No. 16. Rôle created by Risse.

Censuren. See Notices.

Centennial March (Grand Festival March). Written for the Centennial Exposition at Philadelphia in 1876, for which Wagner received through Theodore Thomas $5,200. Full title, "Grand Festival March, for the Opening of the Centennial, Commemorative for the Declaration of Independence of the United States of America. Composed and Dedicated to the Women's Centennial Committees by Richard Wagner."

Chamberlain, Houston Stewart. Born in Southsea, Hampshire, England, Sept. 9, 1855, the son of an Admiral. Son-in-law of Richard Wagner, having married his daughter Eva Dec. 26, 1908, in Bayreuth. He had not known Wagner personally but since 1882 (the first *Parsifal* presentation in Bayreuth) he had been an enthusiastic proclaimer of his—Wagner's— great art. Author of *Richard Wagner*, translated from the German by G. Ainstre Hight, London, J. M. Dent & Co., 1900; *The Wagnerian Drama*, London, J. Lane, 1915. Died Jan. 1927 in Bayreuth.

Choral Works. See Musical Works.

Colonna, Steffano. A character in *Rienzi*; bass. A patrician. Act 1, No. 1; Act 2, Nos. 5, 6, 7. Rôle created by Dettmer.

Columbus Overture. Composed and performed at Magdeburg in 1835. Performed also at Riga in 1838 and at Paris Feb. 4, 1841. Published by Metzler & Co. Score lost.

Communication to My Friends, A. P.W. 1. A quasi-biography written by Wagner while at Zürich in 1851; a story of his artistic development. Throws light upon motives which led to the composition of *Lohengrin.* Of 131 pages, with many autobiographic details. Originally published as a preface to the three opera-poems *Dutchman, Tannhäuser* and *Lohengrin.* In it is the first public announcement of his plan for a Nibelung Festival. It also tells how in Paris (1839-1842) "the German Folk book of Tannhäuser" fell into his hands.

His objective was to explain the apparent contradictions between his opera and his theoretic writings, and give his friends an understanding of him both as man and artist.

Conducting, On. P.W. 4. Published in the *Neue Zeitschrift* Nov. 26, Dec. 3, 10, 17, 24, 1869, Jan. 1, 7, 14, 21, 1870. According to Glasenapp the articles appeared simultaneously in the *New Yorker Musik-Zeitung.* They embody the results of studies and experiences as conductor in the Dresden Theatre. The art of instrumental expression, of orchestral singing, is for the first time formulated in scientific terms.

Crimhilda. Mother of Gunther and Gutrune. In the Volsunga Saga she is said to have been ravished by Alberich and she bore him a natural son, Hagen.

D

Daland. A character in *The Flying Dutchman*; bass. A Norwegian sea-captain. Act 1, scenes 1, 3; Act 2, scene 3; Act 3, scene 2. Rôle created by Risse.

David. A character in *Die Meistersinger*; tenor. Apprentice to Hans Sachs. Acts 1, 2, 3. Rôle created by Schlosser.

Descente de la Courtille, La. A vaudeville to which Wagner wrote the music while in Paris.

Destiny of Opera, The. P.W. 5. Written in 1871. Published by E. W. Fritzch, Leipzig, 1871. Intended as a thesis for his installation as a member of the Royal Academy of the Arts in Berlin on Apr. 28, 1871.

Deutsche Kunst und Deutsche Politik. See German Art and German Policy.

Deutsches Musikwesen, Über. See German Musician in Paris, A, No. 4: On German Music.

Deux Grenadiers, Les. Listed in Musical Works; The Two Grenadiers. (Heine's *Die beiden grenadiere*). Paris, 1839. Dedicated to Heine. Music fits the French version.

Devrient, Eduard. See Notices, No. 4; also next item below.

Devrient's History of German Acting, On E. P.W. 8. Written Jan. 8, 1849. Sent to the Augsburg *Allgemeine Zeitung* but not printed. Printed in 1877 by Ludwig Nohl.

Dich theure Halle. "Thou, dear hall!" Elizabeth's aria in *Tannhäuser*, Act 2, scene 1. She enters the Hall of the Muses overjoyed at the return of Tannhäuser who had disappeared a year previously.

> "Oh, hall of song I give thee greeting!
> All hail to thee, thou hallowed place!"

Dichten und Komponiren, Über das. See Poetry and Composition, On.

Dirigiren, Über das. See Conducting, On.

Donizetti—"Elisir d'amore." Listed in Musical Works. Piano-forte score.

Donizetti—"La Favorita." Listed in Musical Works. Piano-forte score, Paris.

Donner. A character in *The Ring*; baritone-bass. God of thunder. *Das Rheingold*, scenes 2 and 4. Rôle created by Heinrich.

Doré, Paul Gustave. Friend and visitor of Wagner in Paris. French engraver and designer. Born at Strasbourg in 1832. Died Jan. 23, 1883. Celebrated as illustrator of the Bible, *Don Quixote*, Dante's *Inferno* and other works.

Dorn, Heinrich Ludwig Egmont. Noted musician and conductor of Germany. Born at Königsberg, Prussia, Nov. 14, 1804. Music Director of the Court Theatre at Leipzig from 1829 to 1832. From 1849 to 1868 he was conductor of the Royal Opera in Berlin. He came from a well-to-do mercantile family and belonged to the Conservative party, hence at first was antagonistic to Wagner's music but later was his friend. He produced two operas of his own composition at Berlin and Königsberg. Directed a performance of one of Wagner's overtures in B flat major in a Leipzig theatre. Died in Berlin Jan. 10, 1892.

Dors, mon enfant. Listed in Musical Works. See Sleep, My Child.

Dreams. Listed in Musical Works. See Five Poems.

Dresden. Residence of Richard Wagner, No. 7 in the Töpfergasse in 1842. Later, end of July 1842 to spring of 1843, No. 5 in the Waisenhausgasse, near the Seethor. Population 70,000 at that time. Also resided in 1843 at Marienstrasse, No. 9; in autumn of 1843 at No. 6 Ostra-Allee.

Dresden Revolution. The items which formed the basis of charges against Wagner for insurrection activities in May 1849, leading to his flight and exile, as listed by Praeger are:

1. Paper on the *Abolition of the Monarchy* read before the Fatherland Union, dated 16th June 1848.
2. Note to August Röckel: "Return immediately; a premature outbreak is feared." May 1849.
3. Letter to Edward Röckel, March 1851:

    (a) "It was no longer possible to endure the state of things in which we lived."
    (b) "I was present everywhere, actively superintending the bringing in of convoys, etc."
    (c) "I was actively engaged in the revolutionary movement up to its final struggle."

4. His active participation, related by himself to me (Praeger), corroborated by Hainberger's testimony.
5. Max von Weber, son of Carl Maria von Weber, told me (Praeger) that he was Present during the Revolution, and saw Wagner shoulder his musket.

Du Metier de Virtuose et de l'Indépendence des Compositeurs: Fantasie Esthétique d'un Musicien. See German Musician in Paris, A. No. 5. The Virtuoso and the Artist.

Duke Godfrey (or Gottfried). A character in *Lohengrin,* mute. Brother of Elsa.

Dutchman, The. A character in *The Flying Dutchman*; baritone. Captain of a phantom ship. Act 1, scenes 2, 3; Act 2, scene 3; Act 3, scene 2. Rôle created by Wächter.

E

Eichel, Johanna Sophia. Daughter of Gottlob Friedrich Eichel (Master of a charity school at Leipzig). Wife of Gottlob Friedrich Wagner, grand-father of Richard Wagner. Died 1814.

Eigel. A character in *Wieland the Smith*; an archer. Brother to Wieland and Helferich.

Einsam in trüben Tagen. "Oft when the hours were lonely." Elsa's air in *Lohengrin*, Act 1, scene 2. Called upon by the King to reply to the charge made by Telramund, after a pause, as in a trance, she begins
"Lonely, amid my sorrow yearning. . . ."
and tells of a knight in glittering armor, of angelic mien, drawing near.

Eislinger, Ulrich. One of the mastersingers in *Die Meistersinger*; tenor. A grocer. Acts 1, 3. Rôle created by Hoppe.

Elizabeth. A character in *Tannhäuser*; soprano. Niece of the Landgrave of Thuringia. Act 2, scenes 1, 2, 3, 4; Act 3, scenes 1, 3. Rôle created by Johanna Wagner.

Ellis, William Ashton. 1869-1919. Author of several works on Richard Wagner. One of the honorary editors of *The Meister*, the organ of the Wagner Society (England), issued quarterly by Redway. See Bibliography (Ellis and also Glasenapp). Died Jan. 2, 1919.

Elsa of Brabant. A character in *Lohengrin*; soprano. Wedded to Lohengrin. Act 1, scenes 2, 3; Act 2, scenes 2, 4, 5; Act 3, scenes 2, 3. Rôle created by Fräulein Agthe.

End in Paris, An. See German Musician in Paris, A. No. 2.

End of the Patronat-Verein. P.W. 6. Letter to H. v. Wolzogen, editor of the *Bayreuther Blätter.* Written in 1882. Published in that periodical April 1882.

Engel, Der. See Five Poems, No. 1: The Angel.

Entrance of the Gods into Valhalla. Stately and majestic march of Wotan, Donner, Froh and Loge across the rainbow bridge towards the castle built for them by the giants, Fasolt and Fafner, to the accompaniment of the orchestra. Finale of *Das Rheingold.*

Entwurf zur Organisation eines deutschen National-Theatres. See Plan of organization of a German National Theatre, etc.

Epilogischer Bericht über die Umstände und Schicksale, weiche die Ausführung des Bühnenfestspieles *"Der Ring des Nibelungen"* bis zur Veröffentlichung der Dichtung desselben begleiteten. See Epilogue to the "Nibelung's Ring."

Epilogue to the "Nibelung's Ring." P.W. 4. Preface to the public issue of the poem of the Bühnenfestspiel *Der Ring des Nibelungen.* Dated Lucerne Dec. 7, 1871. Put in pamphlet form by Fritzch, Leipzig, 1872, under "Report to the German Wagner Union on the circumstances and fates which have attended the execution of *Der Ring des Nibelungen.*"

Erda. A character in *The Ring*; mezzo-soprano. Goddess of wisdom. *Das Rheingold,* scene 4. Rôle created by Fräulein Seehofer. *Siegfried,* Act 3. Rôle created by Luise Jäide.

Erik. A character in *The Flying Dutchman*; tenor. A huntsman; Senta's lover. Act 2, scenes 1. 2; Act 3, scene 2. Rôle created by Reinhold.

Erinnerungen an Auber. See Auber, Reminiscences of.

Erinnerungen an Spontini. See Spontini, Mementoes of.

Erkenne dich Selbst. See Religion and Art, No. 2: Know Thyself.

Erntefest, Das. Play (serious drama) written by Ludwig Geyer in which his step-daughter Rosalie first appeared on March 2, 1818, in Dresden.

Eschenbach, Wolfram von. See Wolfram von Eschenbach.

Eva. A character in *Die Meistersinger*; soprano. Daughter of Veit Pogner. Acts 1, 2, 3. Rôle created by Fräulein Mallinger.

Evening Star Song. "O du, mein holder Abendstern." Wolfram's air in *Tannhäuser*, Act 3, scene 2. Seated alone, he apostrophizes the evening star: "Oh, blessed star! thou reignest above, and sheddest on us thy mild benignant rays!" accompanying himself on the harp.

Explanatory Programmes. P.W. 3. Written 1852-53.
1. Beethoven's *Heroic Symphony*.
   Published in *Neue Zeitschrift für Musik*, Oct. 15, 1852.
2. Beethoven's Overture to *Coriolanus*.
3. Overture to *Der Fliegende Holländer*.
   Published in *Neue Zeitschrift für Musik*, Aug. 5, 1853.
4. Overture to *Tannhäuser*.
   Published in *Neue Zeitschrift für Musik*, Jan. 14, 1853.
5. Prelude to *Lohengrin*.
   Published in *Neue Zeitschrift für Musik*, June 17, 1853.

F

Fafner. A character in *The Ring*; bass. A giant, later changed into a dragon.
Das Rheingold, Scenes 2, 4. Rôle created by Bausewein.
Siegfried, Act 2. Rôle created by Franz von Reichenberg.

Fantasie, F ♯ minor. Listed in Musical Works. Written 1831. Unpublished.

Fasolt. A character in *The Ring*; baritone-bass. A giant. *Das Rheingold*, scenes 2, 4. Rôle created by Polzer.

Fatherland Union. Revolutionary organization in Saxony to which Wagner and his friend August Röckel belonged.

Fatima. A character in *The Saracen Woman*; soprano.

Faust Ouverture, Eine. See Faust Overture.

Faust Overture. Listed in Musical Works. Written in Paris 1839-40, finished Feb. 4, 1840. The composer termed it an *Overture to Goethe's Faust.* Originally intended as the first movement of a grand *Faust-Symphony.* Rewritten and published 1855. In its original form it was first performed in Dresden on July 22, 1844, at one of the annual charity concerts in the Grosser Garten. Conceived after a rehearsal of Beethoven's Ninth Symphony in the winter of 1839. The orchestra of the Paris Conservatoire tried to rehearse it but failed to master it. Dr. Hans von Bülow in 1860 wrote a pamphlet of thirty-one pages on this work, containing a poetic and technical analysis of this tone-poem. Published by F. Kahnt, Leipzig. The revised overture was first performed Jan. 23, 1855, at Zürich.

Feen, Die (The Fairies). Romantic opera in three
acts, composed by Wagner in 1833 in Würzburg,
finished Dec. 7, 1834. First performed in Munich on
June 29, 1888. Libretto after one of Gozzi's fairy
tales, *La donna serpente* (The serpent woman). Published in the summer of 1851. It was never performed
in the lifetime of the composer. The overture only
was played at Magdeburg 1834. Original score was in
the possession of the King of Bavaria. Detailed ac-
counts of the performance in Munich may be found
in L. C. Evans' *European Reminiscences,* (Chicago,
1891, p. 99-102.)

> "A fairy renounces her immortality for the sake of a man
> whom she loves. She can only become mortal by the observance
> of certain hard conditions on the part of her lover; should he
> fail, she will have to suffer a cruel fate. The ordeal is that
> he shall not lose faith in her or disown her, however wicked
> and cruel she may appear in the part she is forced to assume,
> and he succumbs to it; the fairy is changed to a stone and at
> last released by the wistful singing of her beloved, whom the
> fairy-king now receives, together with his bride, into the im-
> mortal joys of the fairy realm."
>
> *A Communication to My Friends, IV, 313.*[1]

It is constructed on the Italian opera model and
comprises the usual run of arias, scenas, cavatinas, etc.

Feretrio. A character in *The Saracen Woman*; bass.

Ferry, Jules. Friend and visitor of Wagner in Paris.
Born at Saint-Dié, April 5, 1832. Died March 17,
1893. French Premier 1880-81, also in 1883.

Festspielhaus. Theatre, or "festival-playhouse," built
at Bayreuth especially for the Wagner *Nibelung*
dramas. Foundation-stone was laid on May 22, 1872.
The architect was Otto Brückwald, of Leipzig, and
Wagner's principal assistant was Karl Brandt, of
Darmstadt. The scenery for *The Ring* dramas was

[1] Vol. I of Ellis' translation of his Prose Works, published by Kegan
Paul, Trench, Trubner and Co. London. 1892-99.

FESTSPIELHAUS (*Bayreuth*)

designed by Prof. Joseph Hoffmann, of Vienna, and painted by the Brothers Brückner, of Coburg.

The circumstances which led to the choice of Bayreuth, the building of the house and all its arrangements are given by Wagner in the 9th volume of his Collected Writings (*Gesammelte Schriften*); in his final report, down to the founding of the Wagner Societies, and his *The Festival Play House in Bayreuth.*

The first public mention of his plan is in his *A Communication to My Friends* 1851. The construction was financed partly by plans of Carl Tausig, young pianist, and Emil Heckel, music publisher of Mannheim; the former, by selling certificates entitling holders to seats at performances; the latter, by forming Wagner societies. It was aided materially by King Ludwig with a contribution of 200,000 marks. At the cornerstone laying in 1872 there was placed in a zinc encasement a telegram from King Ludwig, which read: "To the Poet-Composer, Richard Wagner, in Bayreuth: To you, dearest friend, I send, from the innermost depths of my heart, my warmest congratulations on this day, so auspicious for the whole of Germany. Blessing and success to the grand enterprise greet you. To-day I am, more than ever, united in spirit with you." Buried beneath the stone was a poetical enigma, by Wagner, as follows:

"Hier schliess ich ein Geheimniss ein,
Da ruh' es viele hundert Jahr!
So lange es verwahrt der Stein,
Macht es der Welt sich offenbar.
    RICHARD WAGNER.

Bayreuth, May 22, 1872."

Translated:

"A secret great I here enclose;
Many hundred years here let it rest!
So long as the stone guards it well,
To the world it will itself reveal."

33

FES-FLO

The first performance of *The Ring* was on August 13, 14, 16, 17, 1876.

In his *Richard Wagner*,[1] W. J. Henderson gives the following description:

"The portion containing the auditorium is small, and about half as high as that containing the stage. Two stages, one above the other, are used, so that while one scene is before the audience the other is preparing in the cellar. The proscenium is extremely plain, and is so contrived that it creates an illusion as to the distance between the audience and the stage. In front of the stage and running partly under it is the pit for the orchestra, so arranged that the musicians are wholly unseen by the audience, and the conductor is visible only to the singers. The auditorium is small and rigorously plain. The parquet seats 1300 persons. Above the last row of seats, and extending all the way across the rear of the auditorium, is a gallery, containing nine boxes for the use of titled visitors. Above this gallery is a second one containing 200 seats. The seating capacity of the entire theatre is about 1500. The parquet seats are arranged in easy curves, so that every person faces the stage and has a perfect view, on the order of the Greek amphitheatre. There are no side seats and no proscenium boxes. The sides of the auditorium are finished with Renaissance columns; and sixteen wide passages, eight on each side, give easy egress from the house. There are no chandeliers. The lighting outfit of the auditorium is just sufficient to enable the audience to find its way about. While the performance is going on, all lights in front of the stage are extinguished."

The festivals are held in July and August; the first summer festival was held in 1883.

The theatre is on a slight eminence, about fifteen minutes' walk from the town, with a fine view. In front is the city, to the right and left the mountain chains of the Fichtelgebirge, behind it a wooded hill on which is a tower of victory, erected after the war with France.

"From Richard Wagner's grave we wend our way to the 'sacred hill' of Bayreuth, on which stands his Festival Theatre. Beautiful parkland with slender birch trees with their silken sheen, and a wealth of flowers herald the approach to the great temple of art, which greets us from the height. Here it was that in 1876 Richard Wagner uttered the proud and prophetic words: 'Here is true art, if you will have it so.' Here

[1] G. P. Putnam's Sons, New York, 1902.

emperors and kings, great men of learning and humble students of art, have received a new revelation, and, enriched and strengthened in mind and soul, they have gone upon their way carrying abroad the fame of the Bayreuth Festival to every civilized country. Thus the name Bayreuth has come to stand for a new ideal in art, and Wagner's works remain an inexhaustible source of spiritual uplift for those who are ready to appreciate them."

> *From a booklet issued by the* Städtisches Verkehrsamt, *Bayreuth.*

See Bayreuth; also Retrospect of the Stage Festivals of 1876, A.

Fir-tree, The. (Der Tannenbaum) Listed in Musical Works. 1838 (Jullien says 1840?[1]) Published 1871.

Fischer, Wilhelm. Stage manager and chorus-master at the Dresden theatre. Bass singer. Also chorus-master at Leipzig. One of Wagner's Dresden friends to whom his letters were written. Died in 1859, aged 69.

See Homage to Ludwig Spohr and Chorus-Master Wilhelm Fischer.

Five Poems. Listed in Musical Works.
1. The Angel (Der Engel).
2. Stand Still (Stehe still).
3. In the Greenhouse (Im Treibhaus); Studies to go with *Tristan and Isolde*.
4. Sorrows (Schmerzen).
5. Dreams (Träume); Studies to go with *Tristan and Isolde*.
1862. English by Francis Hueffer.

Flosshilde. A character in *The Ring*; mezzo-soprano. A Rhine maiden.

> *Das Rheingold*, Scenes 1, 4. Rôle created by Fräulein Ritter.
> *Götterdämmerung*, Act 3. Rôle created by Minna Lammert.

---

[1] *Richard Wagner.* J. B. Millet Co., Boston, 1892.

Flying Dutchman, The. (Der Fliegende Holländer).
Romantic opera in three acts.

CHARACTERS

Daland, a Norwegian sea-captain - -	Bass
Senta, his daughter - - - - - -	Soprano
Erik, a huntsman - - - - - - -	Tenor
Mary, Senta's nurse - - - - - -	Contralto
Mate - - - - - - - - - - -	Tenor
The Dutchman - - - - - - - -	Baritone

Time—18th century

Scene—The Norwegian coast and a Norwegian fishing village.

Original sketch, one act, was made in May 1840. Written at Meudon, near Paris, between May 18 and 28, 1841. The music of the opera was composed in July and August, 1841, and all except the overture was completed in seven weeks. Orchestration score in manuscript form completed in the autumn of 1841. The manuscript of the poem was sold under pressure for £20. It is the first of Wagner's music-dramas. He revised the last 53 measures of the overture in 1860.

SOURCES

It is about a sea-captain who was prevented by contrary winds from rounding the Cape and swore he would succeed even though Hell itself should oppose him. This offended Satan greatly and as punishment he was condemned to sail the seas forever. The only relief permitted was that once in seven years he might land in order to search for a woman who would love him and be faithful to him.

It was inspired by Wagner's tempestuous voyage from Riga to London in 1839 on the "Thetis," a small sailing vessel. Based on H. Heine's version of the legend in his *Salon* as it appeared in *The Memoirs of Herr Schnabelewopski*, where he refers to a play which he had seen at Amsterdam. A version of the ancient legend was printed in *Blackwood's Magazine* in May 1821, as follows:

"She was an Amsterdam vessel and sailed from port seventy years ago. Her Master, Van der Decken, was a stanch seaman, determined to have his own way in spite of the devil, but respected by the sailors under him. The story is that in doubling the Cape they were a long day trying to weather Table Bay. The wind headed them, went against them, and Van der Decken walked the deck swearing at the wind. After sunset a vessel spoke him, asking if he were going into the bay that night. Van der Decken replied 'May I be eternally damned if I do though I should beat about here till judgment day.' He never did enter that bay and it is believed that he still beats about those seas. The vessel is never seen except with foul weather along with her."

THE OPERA

Argument

Act 1

Near the Norwegian coast a Norwegian brig comes in contact with the phantom ship of "The Flying Dutchman." Daland, captain of the Norwegian ship, enters into an agreement with the unknown Dutchman to provide him with a home and Senta, his daughter, in exchange for rich treasures stored in the Dutchman's ship.

Act 2

Senta and her nurse, Mary, together with a group of Norwegian girls are turning their spinning wheels and singing a spinning song. Senta is absorbed in contemplation of a picture of "The Flying Dutchman" hanging on the wall. She sings a ballad sketching a story of the Dutchman and vows that through her his torment will be ended. Erik, Senta's lover, urges his suit and warns her of the fatal termination of her

37

infatuation for the phantom mariner. Daland arrives and presents the Dutchman whom Senta accepts as her affianced husband.

Act 3

The crew of the Norwegian brig try to engage the "Flying Dutchman" crew in merry-making but without avail. Erik again pleads his love to Senta and at this juncture the Dutchman appears and gives orders for departure, on the supposition that Senta is faithless and inconstant in her love for him as all others of her kind have been heretofore. Senta, however, reaffirms her loyalty to him, even after the Dutchman has revealed his identity. "Thine will I be, until death shall us part!" she exclaims and casts herself into the sea.

Produced first at the Royal Saxon Court Theatre, Dresden, on Jan. 2, 1843, with this cast:

Senta - - - - -	Mme. Schröder-Devrient
The Dutchman - -	Wächter
Daland - - - -	Risse
Erik - - - - -	Reinhold
Mary - - - - -	Mme. Wächter
Mate - - - - -	Bielezizky

CONDUCTOR, Richard Wagner

Given at Riga May 22, 1843; and at Zürich, Wagner conducting, in May 1852.

First performance in America as "Il Vascello Fantasma," in Philadelphia, Nov. 2, 1876, by the Pappenheim Company.

First performed in New York at the Academy of Music, Jan. 26, 1877, by the Kellogg English Opera Company.

Cast

Senta - - - - - - Clara Louise Kellogg
The Dutchman - - - W. T. Carleton
Daland - - - - - Mr. Conly
Erik - - - - - - Mr. Turner

Conductor, S. Behrens

First performed in New York in German at the
Academy of Music, March 12, 1877.

Cast

Senta - - - - - Mme. Eugenia Pap-
- penheim
The Dutchman - - - A. Blum
Daland - - - - - Mr. Preusser
Erik - - - - - - Christian Fritsch
Mary - - - - - - Miss Cooney
Steersman (Mate) - - Mr. Lenoir

Conductor, A. Neuendorff

Wagner required that the phantom ship should approach rapidly from the background, instead of coming
slowly and jerkily from one of the wings. Recently the
Munich authorities, by using film projection, show the
ship approaching with great rapidity.

See Explanatory Programmes; Music of the Future;
Remarks on performing the opera "The Flying
Dutchman." For Leading Motives see the appen-
dix, p. 187.

Folz, Hans. One of the mastersingers in *Die Meistersinger*; bass. A coppersmith. Acts 1, 3. Rôle
created by Hayn.

Forest Bird, Voice of the. A character in *The Ring*;
soprano.
Siegfried, Act 2. Rôle created by Lilli Lehmann.

Forging the Sword. Siegfried's air in Act 1 of *Siegfried.* "Nothung! Nothung!"

Frederick of Telramund. A character in *Lohengrin*; baritone. A Count of Brabant and guardian of Elsa; Ortrud's husband. Act 1, scenes 1, 2, 3; Act 2, scenes 1, 2, 3, 5; Act 3, scenes 2, 3. Rôle created by Milde.

Freia. A character in *The Ring*; soprano. Goddess of youth and beauty.
> *Das Rheingold*, Scenes 2, 4. Rôle created by Fräulein Müller.

Freischütz in Paris, Der. P.W. 7.
> First article published in *Gazette Musicale* May 23, 30, 1841. It prepared the Paris public for the performance of the opera on June 7, 1841.
> Second article dated June 20, 1841, in *Abend-Zeitung* July 16, 17, 19, 20, 21, 1841. An account of the performance conveyed to the German public.

Fricka. A character in *The Ring*; soprano. Goddess of marriage; wife of Wotan.
> *Das Rheingold*, Scenes 2, 4. Rôle created by Fräulein Stehle.
> *Die Walküre*, Act 2. Rôle created by Fräulein Kaufmann.

Friedrich der Rothbart. Frederick Redbeard, i.e., Barbarossa. A projected drama, in 1848; abandoned in July. A five-act sketch for a spoken drama. Preserved at Wahnfried. Preliminary sketch dated Oct. 31, 1846.

Froh. A character in *The Ring*; tenor. God of lightning.
> *Das Rheingold*, Scenes 2, 4. Rôle created by Nachbaur.

Fünf Gedichte. See Five Poems.

G

Galvani, Friederike. A resident of Würzburg with whom Wagner had a love affair.

Gaspérini, A. de. One of the biographers of Wagner, friend and visitor of Wagner in Paris. A physician and author. He wrote a biography of the composer of 173 pages, published by Heugel, 1866, Paris.

Gelegenheits Cantate. See Special Cantata.

Geneva. Wagner lodged on the third floor of the "Maison James Fazy," subsequently the Hôtel de Russie, corner of the Quai du Léman and Rue du Montblanc. In the summer of 1856 he boarded not far from the city in a pension, half-way up Mont Salève.

Gerhilde. A character in *The Ring*; soprano with dramatic ability. A valkyrie. *Die Walküre*, Act 3. Rôle created at first Festspielhaus performance by Marie Haupt.

German Art and German Policy. P.W. 4. Published in *Süddeutsche Presse* in 1867 and by J. J. Weber of Leipzig in 1868.

German Music, On. See German Musician in Paris, A. No. 4.

German Musician in Paris, A. P.W. 7. Tales and Articles.

    1.   A Pilgrimage to Beethoven.
        Published in *Revue et Gazette Musicale de Paris,* Nov. 19, 22, 29, Dec. 3, 1840. It attracted the attention of Hector Berlioz. Published first in Germany in the Dresden *Abend-Zeitung* July 30 to Aug. 5, 1841.

2. An End in Paris.
   Published in *Gazette Musicale* Jan. 31, Feb. 7, 11, 1841. First published in German in *Abend-Zeitung* Aug. 6 to 11, 1841.

3. A Happy Evening.
   Published in *Gazette Musicale* Oct. 21, Nov. 7, 1841. A dialogue on the nature of music.

4. On German Music.
   Published in *Gazette Musicale* July 12, 26, 1840.

4a. Pergolesi's *Stabat Mater*.
   Published in *Gazette Musicale* Oct. 11, 1840.

5. The Virtuoso and the Artist.
   Article by Wagner published in the *Gazette Musicale* of Oct. 18, 1840, in which he compared his own independence with the dependence of the virtuoso upon public fancy and shallowness. In Vol. 1, p.217-22 of his *Gesammelte Schriften*. In this he writes an amusing report of a performance of Mozart's *Don Juan* in Paris.

6. The Artist and Publicity.
   Published in *Gazette Musicale* Apr. 1, 1841.

7. Rossini's *Stabat Mater*.
   Published in *Neue Zeitschrift für Musik* Dec. 28, 1841, signed "A. Valentino."

German Opera, On. P.W. 8. Published in Laube's *Zeitung für die elegante Welt* June 10, 1834. Not included in *Gesammelte Schriften*. Said to be the earliest contribution of Wagner to the press.

Gewandhaus. Ancient armory of the city of Leipzig where concerts were held, hence so-called. They date back to 1723-50, when Bach was Cantor of the Thomasschule. Originally called "das grosse Concert."

Here Wagner first heard the works of Beethoven. Wagner's *Concert Ouverture mit Fuge in D minor* was performed here Dec. 25, 1831. His symphony in C major, composed in 1832, was performed on Jan. 10, 1833.

Geyer, Benjamin. (1682-1742) Son of Benjamin Geyer. Organist at St. Andrew's Church, Eisleben, 1703 till his death. Ancestor of Ludwig Geyer.

Geyer, Cäcilie. Daughter of Ludwig Geyer, half-sister of Richard Wagner, wife of Eduard Avenarius. Called Frau Avenarius in Wagner's correspondence.

Geyer, Christian Gottlieb Benjamin. (1744-1799) Son of Gottlieb Benjamin Geyer. Studied law at Leipzig, was advocate and actuary and appointed clerk. Married the daughter of a former cook to a Dresden Commandant.

Geyer, Gottlieb Benjamin. (1710-1762) Son of Benjamin Geyer, the younger. Studied music and philosophy. Married the daughter of the cantor of St. Anne's, Eisleben, about 1737, and later served as cantor of the same church and afterward organist and cantor of St. Nicholas Church.

Geyer, Karl Friedrich Wilhelm. (1791- ?) Son of Christian Gottlieb Geyer. Brother of Ludwig Geyer.

Geyer, Ludwig Heinrich Christian. (1780-1821) Born Jan. 21, 1780, in Eisleben. Son of Christian Gottlieb Benjamin Geyer. His father was Actuary to the Overseer-in-chief. Friend of Richard Wagner's father and the second husband of Wagner's mother. Talented actor, singer, author and portrait painter. He was commissioned to paint the royal families in Munich and in Dresden. He attended the University of Leipzig in order to study law. Once appeared in *Joseph of Egypt* at Dresden when the opera was produced by Weber. Author of *The Slaughter of the Innocents,* well-known in Germany, also of *Der Bethlehemitische Kindermord,* a comedy, published in Reclam's *Universal-bibliothek.* Died Sept. 30, 1821.

Gibich. The name is obtained from the *Lex Burgundiorum* of Gundohar, a Burgundian King of the fifth century, who in it names, as one of his ancestors, Gibica. Derived from the same root as Giuki, the name used in the Volsunga saga.

Gibichungen. A race of heroes, of divine origin, on the Rhine.

Glasenapp, Carl Friedrich. Born Oct. 3, 1847, in Riga. Died in Riga Apr. 14, 1915. Author of *Life of Richard Wagner.* The foundation of every Wagner biography. It has a wealth of material and is very minute but discursive and lacks critical value. The translation by William Ashton Ellis is in six volumes but from vol. 4 on Ellis so broadened the scope and included so little of Glasenapp that the latter's name does not appear on the title page. It brings Wagner's life down to only the 46th year. Glasenapp was professor of the German language and literature at the Polytechnikum at Riga; author of many works about Richard Wagner and Siegfried Wagner. He wrote also for the *Bayreuther Blätter.*

Glory to thee. Tenor's air in *Tannhäuser,* Act 1, scene 2. He sings praises to Venus.

Glückliche Bärenfamilie, Die. See Happy Bear Family, The.

Glücklicher Abend, Ein. See German Musician in Paris, A. No. 3.

Gluck's Iphigénie en Aulide. Listed in Musical Works. An arrangement made by Wagner in 1846. Pianoforte arrangement by H. von Bülow. Published 1859. Score of close to overture published 1859.

Gluck's Overture to Iphigenia in Aulis. P.W. 3. Published in *Neue Zeitschrift* July 1, 1854, together with the new close, arranged by Richard Wagner, now generally used for concert purposes, comprising 33 bars of music.

Gnita Plain. The plain of Discord where the giants in *Das Rheingold* left the treasure and the ring.

Godfrey. See Duke Godfrey.

Goethe Institute, On the. P.W. 3. A letter to Franz Liszt written 1851. Published in the *Neue Zeitschrift für Musik* March 5, 1852.

Goethestiftung, Über die. See Goethe Institute, On the.

Götterdämmerung. See *Ring of the Nibelungs, The*: Twilight of the Gods.

Gollmann, Elise. Wife of Albert Wagner, a brother of Richard. Celebrated for her extensive range of voice; could sing *Tancredi* and *The Queen of the Night* equally well.

Good Friday's Spell. *Parsifal*, Act 3. Parsifal is charmed by the beauty of the landscape:

> How fair the fields and meadows seem to-day!
> Many a magic flower I've seen,
> Which sought to clasp me in its baneful twinings;
> But none I've seen so sweet as here.

GURNEMANZ:
> That is Good Friday's spell, my lord!

> The sad repentant tears of sinners
> Have here with holy rain
> Besprinkled field and plain
> And made them glow with beauty.

Gottfried. See Duke Godfrey.

Gram. A character in *Wieland the Smith.* A Marshal to Neiding, King of the Niaren.

Grane. Brünnhilde's horse; "Grani" of the Volsunga saga.

Great Festival March. See Centennial March.

Green Hill. Name of villa at Enge, suburb of Zürich, owned and occupied by the Wesendoncks.

Greeting from Saxony to the Viennese. P.W. 8. Published in *Allegemeine Österreichische Zeitung* June 1, 1848.

Greeting to the King. Listed in Musical Works. 1844. Published, first, for four male voices and, second, as a song with pianoforte accompaniment. Performed in Dresden Aug. (9?) 12, 1844, on the King of Saxony's return from England.

Grimgerde. A character in *The Ring*; soprano of dramatic quality. A valkyrie.
> *Die Walküre*, Act 3. Rôle created at first Festspielhaus performance by Hedwig Reicher-Kindermann.

Grosser Festmarsch. See Centennial March.

Gruss den König, 1844. See Greeting to the King, 1844.

Guitarrero, Le. A dramatic work in three acts by Halévy, Jan. 21, 1840. Wagner made a piano score at Paris in 1841.

Gunther. A character in *The Ring*; baritone. King of the Gibichungs on the Rhine.
> *Götterdämmerung*, Acts 1, 2, 3. Rôle created by Eugen Gura. Gunnar of Volsunga saga. Gunther in *Nibelungen Lied.* Represented as a weak

person under the influence of others. One of a
race of heroes of divine origin, called the
Gibichungen, on the Rhine. Brother of Gutrune
or Gudrun.

Gurmun. In *Tristan*, an Irish king, brother-in-law to
Morold.

Gurnemanz. A character in *Parsifal*; bass. A veteran
knight of the Grail. Acts 1, 3. Rôle created by
Scaria.

Gutrune. A character in *The Ring*; soprano. Sister
to Gunther.
Götterdämmerung, Acts 1, 2, 3. Rôle created by
Mathilde Weckerlin. Gudrun of Volsunga Saga,
daughter of Grimheld. In *Nibelungen Lied*
Chriemhild is Gutrune; sister of Gunther.

Gutzgow, Carl Ferdinand (or Gutzkow). Author.
Influenced Wagner in his daily life and thought.
Popular German novelist and dramatist. Born in
Berlin in 1811. Published successful tragedies, a
comedy and critical essays. Became a resident of
Dresden in 1847. Died Dec. 16, 1878.

H

Hagen. A character in *The Ring*; bass. Natural son
of Alberich; half-brother to Gunther and Gutrune.
Götterdämmerung, Acts 1, 2, 3. Rôle created by
Gustav Siehr. Son of Grimhild or Crimhilda.
A crafty villain in the *Nibelungen Lied* and
Thidrek Saga, but of a noble nature in the
Volsunga Saga.

Hagenbuch, Franz. Friend in Zürich of Wagner;
deputy cantonal secretary.

Hail bright abode! Freudig begruessen wir die edle Halle. Chorus in *Tannhäuser*, Act 2, scene 4. Entrance of nobles, cavaliers and ladies into the Hall of Muses where the contest of the bards is to be held. "Hail bright abode, where song the heart rejoices!"

Halévy, Jacques François Fromental Elias. French-Jewish composer; real name Lévi. Born in Paris May 27, 1799. Died at Nice Mar. 17, 1862. Author of *La Reine de Chypre* and *Le Guittarrero*.

Halévy—"Le Guittarero." Listed in Musical Works. Pianoforte score, Paris, 1841.

Halévy and "La Reine de Chypre." P.W. 8. Published in *Gazette Musicale* Feb. 27, March 13, Apr. 24, May 1, 1842.

Halévy's "Reine de Chypre." Account of a new Parisian opera. P.W. 7, A report on its first performance Dec. 22, 1841. Published in Dresden *Abend-Zeitung* Jan. 26, 27, 28, 29, 1842. Musical Works: Pianoforte score, Paris, 1841.

Hanslich, Eduard. (1825-1904) Music critic and writer. Author of *The Beautiful in Music*; New York, Novello, Ewer & Co. 1891. Born at Prague, Sept. 11, 1825. Son of a noted bibliographer. He studied law and philosophy, taking the degree of Doctor in 1849 in Vienna. First met by Wagner at Marienbad. A devotee of music and a great admirer of *Rienzi* and the *Dutchman*. As a Conservative in music he became an intense critic of the Liszt-Wagner movement. Died at Baden, near Vienna, Aug. 4, 1904. His life (in German) was published in 1894 at Berlin by the Allegemeine Verein für Deutsche Litteratur. See Beckmesser.

Happy Bear Family, The. A two-act comic opera planned by Wagner at Riga, on a subject suggested by the *Thousand and one Nights*. He composed only two numbers but, becoming disgusted with the character of music which he was being led into, abandoned it. The manuscript was found at Riga in 1872, together with sketches for some of the music. Text is in Vol. XI of his *Collected Works*.

Happy Evening, A. See German Musician in Paris, A. No. 3.

Heine, Heinrich. Celebrated German poet and author, of Jewish extraction. Born at Düsseldorf, Dec. 13, 1799. Died Feb. 17, 1856. Author of *Doctor Faust* and other works. Influenced Wagner in his daily life and thought. His version of the legend of the Flying Dutchman inspired Wagner with the music for that opera.

Heinrich der Schreiber. A character in *Tannhäuser*; tenor. ·A notary. Act 1, scene 4; Act 2, scene 4; Act 3, scene 3. Rôle created by Gurth.

Heinse, Wilhelm (Johann Jakob Wilhelm). German *littérateur*. Born in Thuringia about 1748. He wrote *Ardinghello* in 1787, a romance. Termed by Franz Muncker as "the apostle of the highest artistic and lowest sensual pleasures; amongst all the authors of the last century the one endowed with the warmest enthusiasm and finest comprehension of music." Published translations of Tasso's *Jerusalem Delivered* and of Ariosto's *Orlando*. His works were read with avidity by Wagner. Died in 1803.

Heldenbuch (Book of Heroes). A collection of poems dating from the 12th century or earlier, dealing with the events of the time of Attila and the incursions of the German nations into Rome. Among the personages that appear in this book are: Siegfried, Gudrune, Hagen and others who reappear in the *Nibelungen Lied*.

Heldenthum und Christenthum. See Religion and Art, No. 3. Hero-dom and Christendom.

Helferich. A character in *Wieland the Smith*, a leech. Brother to Wieland and Eigel.

Helmwige. A character in *The Ring*; soprano of dramatic quality. A valkyrie. *Die Walküre*, Act 3. Rôle created at first Festspielhaus performance by Lilli Lehmann.

Henry the Fowler. A character in *Lohengrin*; bass. King of Germany. Act 1, scenes 1, 2, 3; Act 2, scene 5; Act 3, scene 3. Rôle created by Höfer.

Herald (King's). A character in *Lohengrin*; baritone-bass. Act 1, scenes 1, 2, 3; Act 2, scene 3. Rôle created by Pätsch.

Hermann, Landgrave of Thuringia. A character in *Tannhäuser*; bass. Act 1, scene 4; Act 2, scenes 3, 4; Act 3, scene 3. Rôle created by Dettmer. The historical Landgrave flourished about the thirteenth century and organized contests of song on the Wartburg. It is believed that these competitions were not of musicians but of poets.

Hero-dom and Christendom. See Religion and Art, No. 3.

Herwegh, Georg. A German lyric poet. Born at Stuttgart in 1817. Political refugee in Switzerland, after invading Baden. A friend in Zürich of Wagner. A great linguist. He introduced to Wagner the works of Schopenhauer. Died Apr. 7, 1875.

Herzeleide. Mother of Parsifal; wife of King Gamuret.

Hiller, Ferdinand. See Notices, No. 2.

Hochzeit, Die (The Wedding). First opera the libretto of which was begun by Wagner, in Prague and continued in Leipzig, in 1832-33. An autograph of the numbers composed, bearing date of March 1, 1833, presented by Wagner to the Würzburg Musikverein, shows an introduction, a chorus, and a septet (not a sextet as stated in his autobiography). He destroyed the libretto on objection to the theme by his sister Rosalie. The fragments were published in full score in the *Gesamtausgabe* by Breitkopf & Härtel in 1912.

SOURCES

Immermann's *Cardenio und Celinde* (1826).

THE STORY

As given in his autobiography:

"I do not remember where I found the material. A frantic lover climbs to the window of the sleeping-chamber of his friend's bride, wherein she is awaiting the advent of the bridegroom; the bride struggles with the madman and hurls him into the courtyard below, where his mangled body gives up the ghost. During the funeral ceremony the bride, uttering one cry, sinks lifeless on the corpse."

Hörselberg. See Wartburg.

Hoffmann, Ernst Theodor Wilhelm Amadeus. Poet, musician, painter and writer of romances, whose books influenced Richard Wagner's imagination. Author of *Master Martin, the Cooper of Nuremberg*; which contained some roots of *Die Meistersinger*. He set forth the inner nature and secret problems of music and called it the representative and very highest revelation of art. Born at Königsberg, Jan. 24, 1776. Studied music and law at the same time. Died June 25, 1822, of paralysis.

Hohe Braut, Die. A romance by Heinrich T. König, upon the reading of which Wagner drafted a complete sketch of an opera, which was sent to Scribe in Paris but was never heard of again.

Holda. Air by the shepherd to Madonna Holda in *Tannhäuser*, Act 1, scene 3. The goddess Holda, in the German legends, represented the power that controlled the productive forces of the earth, i.e. the Goddess of Spring. At the coming of Christianity she was banished with other heathen deities as personifying evil and a symbol of rather wild pleasures. She became identified with Venus, the source of all evils of the senses.

Homage to Ludwig Spohr and Chorus-Master Wilhelm Fischer. P.W. 3. Published in the *Neue Zeitschrift für Musik* Dec. 2, 1859 under the title "To the memory of my beloved Fischer," dated Paris, Nov. 1859. Apparently written to his friend Ferdinand Heine.

Hoop and Horseshoe. No. 10 Queen St., Tower Hill, stopping place of Wagner in London on his voyage from Russia in 1839. It has disappeared.

Hülsen, Botho von. Born Dec. 10, 1815 at Berlin. In 1880 he was still living. Intendant general at the Royal Opera House in Berlin from 1852.

Huldigungs Marsch. See March of Allegiance.

Human Womanly, The. P.W. 6. As conclusion of *Religion and Art.* Published in 1885. Not included in *Collected Writings.* Commenced two days before his death in Venice.

Hunding. A character in *The Ring*; bass.
    Die Walküre, Acts 1, 2. Rôle created by Bausewein.

I

Im Treibhaus (In the Greenhouse). See Five Poems, No. 3.

In fernem Land (In distant land). Lohengrin's narrative, Act 3, scene 3, in which he tells of the temple on Mount Monsalvat which houses the "Grail," and reveals his own and his father's (Percival's) names.

In the Greenhouse (Im Treibhaus). See Five Poems, No. 3.

Incidental Music to a Fairy Farce by Gleich. Listed in Musical Works. Songs. Title: The Spirit of the Mountain, or the Three Wishes. Magdeburg, 1836. Ellis suggests 1835 as the more likely date. (See *Life*, I, 195). Unpublished. Manuscript probably lost.

Invitation to the Production of "Tristan" in Munich. P.W. 8. Open letter to Friedrich Uhl, editor of the *Wiener Botschafter*, 1865. Reprinted in *Bayreuther Blätter* June, 1890.

Irene. A character in *Rienzi*; soprano. Sister of Cola Rienzi. Act 1, Nos. 1, 2, 3; Act 2, No. 7; Act 4, No. 12; Act 5, Nos. 14, 15. Rôle created by Fräulein Wüst.

Isolde. A character in *Tristan and Isolde*; soprano. An Irish princess. Act 1, scenes 1, 2, 3, 4, 5, 6, 7; Act 2, scenes 1, 2, 3; Act 3, scenes 1, 2, 4. Rôle created by Mme. Schnorr von Carolsfeld.

Isot. In *Tristan*, wife of King Gurmun.

Isot of the White Hand. In *Tristan*, daughter of the Duke of Sussex.

Isot the Fair (Isolde). In *Tristan*, daughter of Queen Isot.

J

Jesus of Nazareth. P.W. 8. A music-drama of five acts, by Wagner. Written between Nov. 1848 and early 1849. The material for the play of 100 pages was published at Leipzig in 1887 by Breitkopf & Härtel, with a dedication by Herr Siegfried Wagner "to the memory of Heinrich von Stein." It contained some of the germs of *Parsifal*.

Jockey Club, Paris. Famous for having drowned out the first performance in Paris of *Tannhäuser* by using hunting whistles, because of dissatisfaction with arrangement for the ballet.

Jottings on the Ninth Symphony. P.W. 8. Published in *Dresdener Anzeiger*, March 24, 31, Apr. 2, 1846.

Judaism in Music. P.W. 3. Published in the *Neue Zeitschrift für Musik*, Sept. 3, 6, 1850. The chief argument was that the Jews were not an artistic people.

K

Kaisermarsch. Listed in Musical Works: Kaiser March. Written 1871.

Kapitulation, Eine. See Capitulation, A.

King Ludwig II. Friend and benefactor of Wagner. Born at Nymphenburg August 25, 1845. Ascended the Bavarian throne March 10, 1864, succeeding his father Maximilian II. He first heard Wagner's works in Munich. He became insane and committed suicide by drowning in Lake Starnburg on June 14, 1886.
See To the Kingly Friend; Poems.

King Marke. See Marke.

King's Herald, The. See Herald (King's).

Klindworth, Karl. Born Hanover Sept. 25, 1830. Died near Berlin in 1916. Last of the great protagonists of Wagner. Author of a great edition of Chopin's pianoforte works; also of pianoforte scores of *The Ring* which are esteemed the best transcriptions. Siegfried Wagner married Mrs. Klindworth's second cousin, Winifred Williams, an English girl whom Mr. Klindworth had adopted.

Klingsor. A character in *Parsifal*; bass. A magician, the great enemy of Good. Act 2. Rôle created by Hill. Historically, a celebrated German poet of the thirteenth century.

Know Thyself. See Religion and Art, No. 2.

König, Gustav. Author. Influenced Wagner in his daily life and thought.

König, Heinrich Joseph. Author of *Die Hohe Braut.* German novelist. Born at Fulda in 1790. Died in 1869.

Königsberg. Wagner was musical director at the Königsberg Theatre in January, 1837. Here was written the overture *Rule Britannia.* The theatre failed in the Spring of 1837.

Kothner, Fritz. One of the mastersingers in *Die Meistersinger*; bass. A baker. Acts 1, 3. Rôle created by Fischer.

Kraft-Liedschen (1871), (Kraft-Song of Strength). Listed in Musical Works. Written April 22, 1871. A little humorous vote of thanks to Herr Ludwig Kraft of Leipzig. Printed in Mueller v. der Werra's *Reichscommersbuch.*

Kundry. A character in *Parsifal*; soprano. Acts 1, 2, 3. Rôle created by Materna. A strange creature, half witch, half penitent, who changes her shape at will. She is a devoted servant of the Grail though under the evil influence of Klingsor.

Kunst und Klima. See Art and Climate.

Kunst und die Revolution, Die. See Art and Revolution.

Künstler und die Öffentlichkeit, Der. See German Musician in Paris, A, No. 6: The Artist and Publicity.

Künstler und Kritiker. See Artist and Critic.

Kunstwerk der Zukunft, Das. See Art-work of the Future, The.

Kurwenal. A character in *Tristan and Isolde*; baritone. One of Tristan's retainers. Act 1, scenes 2, 4, 5, 7; Act 2, scene 3; Act 3, scenes 1, 3, 4. Rôle created by Mitterwurzer.

L

Lancia. A character in *The Saracen Woman*; bass.

Landgrave. See Hermann, Landgrave of Thuringia.

Laube, Heinrich. Born at Schrottau in Silesia in 1806. German poet and *litterateur*. Author of *Das junge Europa*, read with avidity by Wagner. Friend and later enemy of the composer. First became acquainted with Wagner on the latter's return from Prague. Wrote the first public criticism of his youthful symphony in C major in *Zeitung für die elegante Welt*, Leipzig, of which he was editor. Died at Vienna, August 1, 1884.

Laussot, Jessie. Friend of Wagner in Zürich, visiting the Ritters. Born in America, married a wine merchant in Bordeaux. An admirer of Wagner and a musician. Became so closely associated with the composer in Paris from early in 1850 to April of that year as to incur the enmity of her husband, Eugene. Wagner finally broke with her and returned to Minna.

Leading Motives (Leit-Motifs). The Wagnerian system of leading motives, or themes with a specified meaning, and purely scenic music such as the "Waldweben" of Siegfried. The musical phrase conveying a particular meaning or thought is repeated by the orchestra as an identifying theme. First employed in *The Flying Dutchman* and later extensively in the music-dramas, especially *The Ring*. The term was first used by Hans von Wolzogen in his *Thematischer Leitfäden*. Arthur Smolian, a German, lists some thirty-three motives in *Tannhäuser* in a pamphlet of which W. A. Ellis made a translation, published by Chappell & Co., London, 1891.

Many of the principal motives (motifs) will be found in the appendix, p. 187.

Lebald. A gigantic work undertaken by Wagner at the age of 14, begun in Dresden; a tragedy on a vast scale, being a mixture of *Hamlet, Richard III, King Lear, Macbeth,* Goethe's *Götz von Berlichingen,* Kleist and other sources, in which there were twenty-two principal characters of which a majority died and had to be brought back as ghosts.

Leipzig. Largest city in Saxony, 64 miles from Dresden. Foremost in the book-selling and publishing trade of Europe. About 800,000 inhabitants. Richard Wagner was born in "The House of the White and Red Lion," No. 88 House Brühl in the

Jewish quarter. This house was demolished in 1885. A tablet marking the date of his birth has been placed on a house which has been erected near the same spot.

Leipzig, University of. Wagner attended lectures on aesthetics and philosophy at this university.

Leit-motif ("Guiding theme"). See Leading Motives, also appendix, p. 187. The term was first used by Hans von Wolzogen in his *Thematischer Leitfäden.*

Letter to H. v. Stein. P.W. 6. Published in *Bayreuther Blätter,* 1883.

Letter to H. v. Wolzogen. See End of the Patronat-Verein.

Letter to Hector Berlioz, A. P.W. 4. This appeared in the *Presse Théatrale* Feb. 26, 1860. German translation published in *Neue Zeitschrift für Musik* Mar. 2, 9, 1860.

Letters. To Dresden friends, Uhlig, Fischer and Heine. Published in three volumes by Breitkopf & Härtel, Leipzig; English versions published by Chas. Scribner's Sons. See Bibliography.

Letters and Minor Essays. P.W. 5.
1. Letter to an Actor.
2. A Glance at the German Operatic Stage of Today. Published in *Musikalisches Wochenblatt* Jan. 1873.
3. Letter to an Italian Friend (Arrigo Boito) on the Production of *Lohengrin* at Bologna. Published in *Norddeutsche Allgemeine Zeitung* 1871.
4. To the Burgomaster of Bologna. Published in *Musikalisches Wochenblatt* Nov. 1872.
5. To Friedrich Nietzsche, Professor of Classical Philology at the University of Bâle.
6. On the Name "Musikdrama."

58

7. Prologue to the Reading of the *Götterdämmerung* before a select audience in Berlin.

   Nos. 6 and 7 were published in *Musikalisches Wochenblatt* Oct. 1872 and March 1873, respectively.

Letters from Paris. P.W. 8. 1841. Published in Dresden *Abend-Zeitung* March, May, June, August, October, December 1841, January 1842. Last in series published in *Neue Zeitschrift für Musik* Feb. 22, 1842. Not included in *Gesammelte Schriften.*

Leubald, ein Trauerspiel. See Lebald.

Liebeslied, Siegmund's. Love song of Siegmund in *Die Walküre*, Act 1. Otherwise called "Spring Song," also "Winterstürme" from the opening word.

Liebesmahl der Apostel, Das. See Love Feast of the Apostles, The.

Liebestod (Love-death). Sung by Isolde over the dead body of Tristan in the finale of *Tristan and Isolde.*

Liebesverbot, Das (Ban or veto on love). Full title, *Das Liebesverbot, or the Novice of Palermo.* Opera in two acts composed in 1834-36; sketched at Teplitz; score written in Magdeburg; finished 1835-36. First and only performance of the opera was in that city on March 29, 1836, under Wagner's direction. Score presented to King Ludwig 1866 with a dedication. Vocal score first published in 1922; full score in 1923.

SOURCES

The subject was taken from Shakespeare's *Measure for Measure.* Its purpose was to demolish "puritanical hypocrisy" and "exalt unrestrained sensuality."

LIE-LOG

Wagner says (*Art, Life and Theories of Richard Wagner*, by E. L. Burlingame [1]):

"Recollections of the 'Sicilian Vespers' [history] may have had something to do with it; and . . . the gentle Sicilian Bellini may also be counted among the factors of this composition. . ."

THE STORY

In a *Communication to My Friends* (P.W. 1) Wagner writes:

"It was Isabella that inspired me; she who leaves her novitiate in the cloister to plead for her brother, who in pursurance of a draconic edict, has been condemned to death for entering on a forbidden, yet nature-hallowed, love-bond with a maiden. Isabella's chaste soul urges on the stony judge such cogent reasons for pardoning the offence, her agitation helps her to paint these reasons in such entrancing warmth of colour that the stern protector of morals is himself seized with passionate love for the superb woman. This sudden, flaming passion proclaims itself by his promising the pardon of the brother as the price of the lovely sister's favours. Aghast at this proposal, Isabella takes refuge in artifice to unmask the hypocrite and save her brother. The Stateholder, whom she has vouchsafed a fictitious indulgence, still thinks to withhold the stipulated pardon so as not to sacrifice his stern judicial conscience to a passing lapse from virtue. Shakespeare disentangles the resulting situation by means of the public return of the Duke, who had hitherto observed events from under a disguise; his decision is an earnest one, and grounded on the judge's maxim, 'measure for measure.' I, on the other hand, unloosed the knot without the Prince's aid by means of a revolution. The scene of action I transferred to the capital of Sicily, in order to bring in the Southern heat of blood to help me with my scheme; I also made the Stateholder, a Puritanical German, forbid a projected carnival; while a madcap youngster, in love with Isabella, incites the populace to mask and keep their weapons ready: 'Who will not dance at our behest, your steel shall pierce him through the breast!' The Stateholder, himself induced by Isabella to come disguised to their rendezvous, is discovered, unmasked, and hooted, the brother in the nick of time is freed by force from the executioner's hands; Isabella renounces her novitiate and gives her hand to the young leader of the carnival. In full procession the maskers go forth to meet their home-returning Prince, assured that he will at least not govern them so crookedly as had his deputy."

[1] H. Holt & Co., New York, 1875.

60

See Burlingame's *Art, Life and Theories of Wagner,*
p.27-40, for an English version of the opera. Score
is preserved at the Munich Opera House.
See also P.W. 7. Account of a first operatic performance. Apparently an extract from Richard
Wagner's Memoirs. Published in Vol. I of *Collected
Writings.*

Liedertafel. Foremost of Dresden choral unions.
Founded in 1839. Wagner was for a time its leader.

Liszt, Franz (Ferencz). Famous pianist and composer and conductor. Conductor at Weimar, friend
and benefactor of Wagner. Born Oct. 22, 1811 at
Raiding in Hungary. Son of Adam Liszt, a court
steward. Princess Karolyne zu Sayn-Wittgenstein
united her life with his in 1847. Brought out at
Weimar *Lohengrin, Tannhäuser* and *The Flying
Dutchman.* Wagner met Liszt for the first time on
his earliest visit to Paris. Liszt died July 31, 1886,
at Bayreuth during the festival season, following the
death, a few days earlier, of Ludwig II. A chapel
built above his grave (designed by Siegfried Wagner)
is inscribed with the words: "Ich weiss dass mein
erloser lebt" (I know that my Redeemer liveth). In
the cemetery are also buried Jean Paul, Dr. Hans
Richter, Houston Stewart Chamberlain, Siegfried
Wagner and Hans Schemm.

Liszt's Symphonic Poems, On Franz. P.W. 3. A
letter to the daughter of Princess Wittgenstein. Written Feb. 15, 1857, from Zürich. Published in the
Neue Zeitschrift April 10, 1857.

Liszt's Symphonische Dichtungen, Über. Brief to
M.W. See Liszt's Symphonic Poems, On Franz.

Loge. A character in *The Ring*; tenor. God of fire.
Das Rheingold, Scenes 2, 3, 4. Rôle created by Vogl.

Logier, Johann Bernard. (1777-1846) Author of *Thoroughbass,* a treatise on harmony and counterpoint, the first musical textbook studied by Wagner in 1828, which he tried to learn in a week. Logier was born at Kassel. His father and grandfather were organists. He invented a machine for guiding the hands of learners on the pianoforte and devised the Logier system. He retired in 1826 and settled in Dublin.

Lohengrin. A character in *Lohengrin;* tenor. Son of King Percival (or Parzival), keeper of the cup known as the "Holy Grail." Act 1, scene 3; Act 2, scene 5; Act 3, scenes 2, 3. Rôle created by Beck.

Lohengrin. Romantic opera in three acts.

CHARACTERS

Henry the Fowler, King of Germany - - - - - -	Bass
Lohengrin - - - - - - -	Tenor
Elsa of Brabant - - - - -	Soprano
Duke Godfrey, her brother -	Mute
Frederick of T e l r a m u n d, Count of Brabant - - -	Baritone
Ortrud, his wife - - - -	Mezzo-soprano
King's Herald - - - - -	Baritone-bass

TIME—First half 10th century

SCENE—Antwerp.

First drafts were made at Marienbad in the summer of 1845 and poem written at Dresden in the same year. Composition of music begun at Grosgraufen, near Pilnitz, in 1846. Third act begun Sept. 9, 1846 and finished March 5, 1847; first act, May 12 to June 8; second act, June 18 to Aug. 2, 1847. Prelude completed Aug. 28, 1847. Orchestration finished by March, 1848. The score was sold to Breitkopf & Härtel for a few hundred thalers. Pianoforte arrangement by Uhlig.

The finale of the first act was performed on Sept. 22, 1848, at Dresden.

The opera was first performed at the Court Theatre, Weimar, on Aug. 28, 1850, the birthday of Goethe, (Wagner not being present) under Liszt.

CAST

Lohengrin - - - - - Beck
Telramund - - - - - Milde
King Henry - - - - - Höfer
Herald - - - - - - Pätsch
Ortrud - - - - - - Fräulein Fastlinger
Elsa - - - - - - - Fräulein Agthe

First performed in America in German at the Stadt Theatre, New York, April 3, 1871, under Adolf Neuendorff.

CAST

Lohengrin - - - - Theodore Habelmann
Telramund - - - - Herr Vierling
King Henry - - - Herr Franosch
Herald - - - - - W. Formes
Ortrud - - - - - Mme. Frederici
Elsa - - - - - - Mme. Louise Lichtmay

It was heard for the first time by Wagner at Vienna on May 15, 1861. Wagner, in May 1853, conducted an orchestra in a concert series at Zürich when selections from the opera were given.

Given in Paris 61 times between Sept. 16, 1891 and Sept. 16, 1892, with receipts of over a million francs.

SOURCES

A version of the story of Lohengrin is contained in the *Parzifal* of Wolfram von Eschenbach. Other sources of Wagner's poem were *Der Jüngere Titurel*, a poem by Albrecht von Schauffenberg; *Der*

Schwanen-Ritter, by Konrad von Würzburg; *Lohen-grin*, a poem by an unknown Bavarian poet; and the *Deutsche Sagen* by Grimm Brothers. See also Muncker's Wagner biography or an article by Muncker in the Munich *Allgemeine Zeitung* for May 30, 1891.

THE OPERA

Argument

Act I

Henry I, King of Germany ("The Fowler"), has arrived at Antwerp to enlist a force to aid him in repelling the Hungarians who have threatened to invade his dominions. The Duchy of Brabant is in a state of anarchy. The late Duke has left his young son Godfrey (or Gottfried) as heir to the throne, who with his sister Elsa are under the guardianship of Count Frederick of Telramund. The Count has fallen in love with Elsa but, having been refused her hand in marriage, married Ortrud, daughter of Radbod, Prince of Friesland, and in right of his wife claims to be the ruler of the Duchy. Godfrey has disappeared and Telramund accuses Elsa of murdering him in order to favor her secret lover whom she hopes to place upon the throne. In reality Ortrud has decoyed Godfrey into a forest and, through her power of enchantment, caused him to take the form of a swan. She informed her husband that she saw Elsa drown her brother in a pool.

Elsa, summoned by the King, makes no defense and it is agreed that the cause should be decided by a combat between Frederick and any champion who may present himself on behalf of the accused. When Elsa has almost lost hope a knight, Lohengrin, appears, ascending the River Scheldt in a boat drawn by a swan. Upon alighting he undertakes her defense. Elsa promises that if he is victorious she will bestow her hand upon him and agrees to his requirement that she shall never ask his name or his origin. Lohengrin strikes Telramund to the ground in the ensuing combat and thus deprives him of his title and estate.

Act II

While preparations are being made for the wedding and while reveling is going on in the *Pallas*, the abode of the knights, Ortrud and Frederick plot revenge and try to devise a way whereby they may regain their lost honors. Approaching the *Kemenate*, or abode of the ladies, through compassion Ortrud moves Elsa to promise to obtain pardon for Frederick and persuades her to listen to the suggestion that she should inquire into the name and origin of her future husband.

As the marriage procession proceeds to the cathedral, Frederick and Ortrud show themselves in their true characters, Ortrud opposing Elsa and Frederick charging the unknown knight is a sorcerer. They are expelled by the King and populace and the marriage takes place.

Act III

After the marriage, goaded by the evil suggestions of Ortrud, Elsa unwisely begins to question Lohengrin in spite of her promise not to do so. At this juncture Frederick enters the room intending to assault his former antagonist and is slain at once by the knight. On the following morning Lohengrin reveals his identity in the presence of the King. He is indebted to the Grail for his invisible power and since his name is now disclosed he can no longer remain in Brabant. The swan returns with the boat to take him away. He removes a gold chain from the neck of the swan and in its place appears Elsa's young brother Godfrey who is now acclaimed rightful Duke of Brabant. Lohengrin departs to the intense grief of his bride, the King and the people.

Wagner's own interpretation of the Prelude is briefly as follows:

"Out of the clear blue ether of the sky there seems to condense a wonderful yet at first hardly perceptible vision; and out of this there gradually emerges, ever more and more clearly, an angel-host bearing in its midst the sacred Grail. As it approaches earth, it pours out exquisite odours, like streams of gold, ravishing the senses of the beholder. The glory of the vision grows and grows until it seems as if the rapture must be shattered and dispersed by the very vehemence of its own expansion.

The vision draws nearer, and the climax is reached when at last the Grail is revealed in all its glorious reality, radiating fiery beams and shaking the soul with emotion. The beholder sinks on his knees in adoring self-annihilation. The Grail pours out its light on him like a benediction, and consecrates him to its service; then the flames gradually die away, and the angel-host soars up again to the ethereal heights in tender joy, having made pure once more the hearts of men by the sacred blessing of the Grail."

Liszt's essay, in his *Collected Writings* III 2, p.141-4, is the classical appreciation:

"To anyone who has neither seen nor heard Wagner's scores, neither studied their consummate workmanship, nor felt their scenic power, it is not as easy to convey a notion of his extraordinary doubling of the great symphonist with the great dramatist."

On the division of the orchestra into three main constituent bodies, with subsidiary groups of three, he says:

"This ternary system has the advantage, among other things, that the whole chord can be given and held in the same scale of colour. Wagner also makes use of a distribution of the strings into separate bodies. In a word, instead of treating the orchestra as an almost homogeneous mass, he parts it into tributary streams and brooks; at times—to change the metaphor—he spins it to the finest parti-coloured threads, and casts their spools first here, then there, now weaving them together, now dividing, until their wondrous ravelling has formed a tissue of most priceless lace. Even in his earlier operas Wagner had always mixed a separate palette for each of his chief characters; but pre-eminently in *Lohengrin*. The more attentively you examine this last score of his, the more you are struck by the intimate relation he has established between his poem and his orchestra. Not only does he personify in rhythms and melodies the feelings and the passions drawn, but animates their contours by a corresponding scheme of colour. Thus the motiv figured in the Prelude and recurring whenever the Holy Grail is thought of, is invariably entrusted to the violins. Elsa is almost exclusively accompanied by the wood-wind, producing the happiest contrasts whenever they follow or are followed by the brass. A peculiarly entralling moment is that after the scene of the long recital for the King, whose rôle is insistently accompanied by regal trumpets and trombones: a silence follows, melting into the softest sigh, like that of a wave just kissed by a breath from heaven: we are under the spell of Elsa's virgin purity, even before herself appears. The selfsame quality of sound descends like dew to quench the ravening flames of the scene between Friedrich and Ortrud, so soon as Elsa steps upon the balcony. It further serves for the bridal procession, and paints so vividly the simple bliss of innocence, as to make this one of the most perfect scenes in all the opera."

See Explanatory Programmes; Music of the Future. For Leading Motives see the appendix, p. 187.

London. On arriving from Riga in 1839 Wagner stopped for a night at the "Hoop and Horseshoe," No. 10 Queen Street, Tower Hill; then lived at a little hotel or boarding house, the King's Arms, in Old Compton Street, Soho.

On his visit to conduct concerts in 1855, arriving Sunday, March 4, 1855, he stopped at 31 Milton Street, Dorset Square; renamed Balcombe Street, a continuation north of Great Quebec Street. He moved to 22 Portland Terrace, Regent's Park. A complete account of Wagner's visit is given by F. Praeger in his *Wagner as I Knew Him.*

London Philharmonic Concerts. Eight concerts held in 1855, Wagner's fee £200. He was obtained as conductor by G. F. Anderson, Director of the Philharmonic Society, although Praeger laid claim to that credit too.

First Concert
March 12, 1855

Part I

Sinfonia, No. 7 (Grand) - - - - - - - - Haydn
Terzetto, "Soave sia il vento" - - - - - Mozart
   (Clara Novello, Mr. and Mrs. Weiss)
Dramatic Concerto (violin, Herr Ernst) - - Spohr
Scena, "Ocean, thou mighty monster!" - - Weber
   (Clara Novello)
Overture, "The Isles of Fingal" - - - - - Mendelssohn

Part II

Sinfonia Eroica - - - - - - - - - - Beethoven
Duet, "O my father" - - - - - - - - Marschner
   (Mr. and Mrs. Weiss)
Overture, "Zauberflöte" - - - - - - - Mozart

Second Concert
March 26, 1855

Part I

Overture, "Der Freischütz" - - - - - - Weber
Aria, "O salutaris Hostia" - - - - - - Cherubini
   (Mrs. Lockey)
Concerto, Violin - - - - - - - - - - Mendelssohn
   (Mr. Blagrove)
Selection from "Lohengrin"
   Introduction, instrumental; Bridal Proces-
   sion; Wedding music and Epithala-
   mium - - - - - - - - - - - - - Wagner

Part II

Choral Symphony, No. 9 - - - - - - - Beethoven

Third Concert
April 16, 1855

Part I

Sinfonia in A, No. 2 - - - - - - - - Mendelssohn
Aria, "Va s'bramando (Faust) - - - - - Spohr
   (Mr. Weiss)

Concerto, Pianoforte, in B flat, Op. 19 - - Beethoven
    (Mr. Lindsay Sloper)
Aria, "Bald schlägt die Abscheidsstunde" - - Mozart
    (Madame Rudersdorff)
Overture, "Euryanthe" - - - - - - - - Weber

Part II

Sinfonia in C minor, No. 5 - - - - - - Beethoven
Recit. "Im Wechsel immer da"
Aria, "Ja, ich fühl'es" (Faust) - - - - - Spohr
    (Mme. Rudersdorff)
Overture, "Les deux Journées" - - - - - Cherubin

Fourth Concert
April 30, 1855

Part I

Sinfonia in B flat, No. 3 MS. - - - - - Lucas
Romanza, "Più bianca" (Les Huguenots) - Meyerbeer
    (Herr Reichardt)
Nonetto for violin, viola, violoncello, contra-
basso, flute, oboe, clarinet, horn and bas-
soon - - - - - - - - - - - - - - Spohr
    (Messrs. Sainton, Hill, Lucas, Howell,
    Pratten, Nicholson, Williams, C.
    Harper and Baumann)
Recit. "A qual furor"
Aria, "O tu, la cui dolce possanza"
  (Fidelio) - - - - - - - - - - - Beethoven
    (Madame Clara Novello)
Overture, "Ruler of the Spirits" - - - - Weber

Part II

Sinfonia, No. 7 - - - - - - - - - - Beethoven
Duetto, "Fra gl'amplessi" (Cosi fan Tutte) - Mozart
    (Madame Clara Novello and
    Herr Reichardt)
Overture, "L'Alcalde de la Vega" - - - - Onslow

Fifth Concert
May 15, 1855

Part I

Sinfonia in E flat - - - - - - - - - Mozart
Aria, "Agitato" (I Fuorus citi) - - - - - Paer
    (Signor Belletti)

Concerto in E minor, Pianoforte - - - - Chopin
    (Mr. C. Hallé)
Aria, "Martern aller Arten" (Die Entfüh-
rung aus dem Serail) - - - - - - - - Mozart
    (Mlle. Jenny Ney, by kind permis-
    sion of the Directors of the
    Royal Italian Opera)
Overture, "Tannhäuser" - - - - - - - Wagner

Part II

Sinfonia Pastorale - - - - - - - - - Beethoven
Romanza, "Roberto! O du den ich liebe"
    (Robert le Diable) - - - - - - - - Meyerbeer
    (Mlle. Jenny Ney)
Barcarola, "Sulla poppa del mio brik" (La
    prigione di Edinburgo) - - - - - - Ricci
    (Signor Belletti)
Overture, "Preciosa" - - - - - - - - Weber

Sixth Concert

May 28, 1855

Part I

Sinfonia in G minor (Manuscript composed
    for the Philharmonic Society [1834]) - - Potter
Aria, "Questi avventurieri" (Seraglio) - - Mozart
    (Herr Formes)
Concerto, violin - - - - - - - - - Beethoven
    (M. Sainton)
Siciliana - - - - - - - - - - - - Pergolesi
    (Mlle. Bockholtz Falconi)
Overture, "Leonora" - - - - - - - - Beethoven

Part II

Sinfonia in A minor, No. 3 - - - - - - Mendelssohn
Recit. "Crudele!"
Aria, "Non mi dir!" (Don Giovanni) - - Mozart
    (Mlle. Bockholtz Falconi)
Recit. "I rage!"
Aria, "O ruddier than the cherry" - - - Handel
    (Herr Formes)
Overture, "Berg-geist" - - - - - - - Spohr

SEVENTH CONCERT
June 11, 1855

Part I

Overture, "Chevy Chase" - - - - - - Macfarren
Aria, "Di militari onori" (Jessonda) - - Spohr
    (Signor Belletti)
Sinfonia Jupiter - - - - - - - - - Mozart
Scena, "Ocean, thou mighty monster"
    (Oberon) - - - - - - - - - - Weber
      (Mme. Clara Novello)
    (Clarinet obbligato, Mr. Williams)
Overture, "Tannhäuser" - - - - - - Wagner

Part II

Sinfonia, No. 8 - - - - - - - - - - Beethoven
Aria, "Ave Maria" - - - - - - - - Cherubini
    (Mme. Clara Novello)
    (Clarinet obbligato, Mr. Williams)
Duetto, "Quel sepolcro" (Agnese) - - - Paer
    (Mme. Clara Novello and
      Signor Belletti)
Overture, "Anacreon" - - - - - - - Cherubini

EIGHTH CONCERT
June 25, 1855

Part I

Sinfonia in C minor, No. 3 - - - - - - Spohr
Scena, "Wie nahte mir der Schlummer
    (Freischütz) - - - - - - - - - Weber
    (Mlle. Emilie Krall of Vienna)
Concerto in A flat Pianoforte - - - - - Hummel
    (Herr Pauer)
Song, "The Spirit Song" - - - - - - Haydn
    (Miss Dolby)
Overture, "Midsummer Night's Dream" - Mendelssohn

Part II

Sinfonia in B flat, No. 4 - - - - - - Beethoven
Duetto, "Della Mosa" (Le Prophète) - - Meyerbeer
    (Mlle. Krall and Miss Dolby)
Overture, "Oberon" - - - - - - - - Weber

Love Feast of the Apostles, The. Composition of
Wagner for three choirs of male voices and orchestra.

71

Made for a festival of the Liedertafel, a vocal society in Dresden presided over by Dr. Loewe with Wagner as leader. Performed July 6 or 7, 1843. Its subject is the Pentecostal descent of the Holy Ghost. A syllabus of the *Liebesmahl* was found on the back of the manuscript of Wagner's article on Mendelssohn's *Saint Paul*. Here it was named the "Gastwahl." Dated April 21, 1843. It was not composed or performed until two or three months later. See Prose Sketch for The Apostles Love Feast.
Musical Works: The Love Feast of the Apostles.

Lüttichau, August Freiherr von. General Director of the Dresden Court Theatre. Replaced von Könneritz in 1824 and held his position until 1862. Formerly Master of Woods and Forests in the Government service.

M

Mädchen aus der Fremde, Das. Comedy written by Ludwig Geyer.

Madonna Holda. Shepherd's air in *Tannhäuser*, Act 1, scene 3. See Holda.

Magdalena. A character in *Die Meistersinger*; mezzo-soprano. Eva's nurse. Acts 1, 2, 3. Rôle created by Frau Diez.

Magdeburg. Wagner was conductor of a small operatic theatre in Magdeburg. Here he resided at No. 2 Margarethengasse, afterward removing to the fourth floor of J. G. Knevel's house, No. 34 Breiterweg, where he remained from 1835 to 1836.

Magic Fire Music. End of Act 3, *Die Walküre*. Music which accompanies the raising of a ring of fire by

Loge at the behest of Wotan, to surround and protect Brünnhilde as she is put to sleep on the mountain rock.

Man and Established Society. P.W. 8. Published in Röckel's *Volksblätter* Feb. 10, Apr. 8, 1849.

Manfred. A character in *The Saracen Woman*; tenor.

Männerlist grösser als Frauenlist, oder Die glückliche Bärenfamilie. See Happy Bear Family, The.

March of Allegiance. Listed in Musical Works. Written 1864 in honor of his patron the King of Bavaria; published 1869. Original score, for a military band, remains in MS. Published version for full orchestra begun by Wagner and finished by Raff.

Marienbad. Wagner spent the summer of 1844 in this city, where he made the first drafts of *Die Meistersinger* and *Lohengrin*.

Marke. A character in *Tristan and Isolde*; bass. King of Cornwall. Act 2, scene 3; Act 3, scene 4. Rôle created by Zottmayer.

Mary. A character in *The Flying Dutchman*; contralto. Senta's nurse. Act 2, scene 1; Act 3, scene 2. Rôle created by Mme. Wächter.

Mastersingers of Nuremberg. See under Meistersinger.

Mate, The. A character in *The Flying Dutchman*; tenor. Mate of Daland's vessel. Act 1, scenes 1, 3; Act 3, scene 1. Rôle created by Bielezizky.

Mein lieber Schwan (My beloved swan). Lohengrin's air in Act 1, scene 3; Act 3, scene 3.

Meine Erinnerungen an Ludwig Schnorr von Carolsfeld. See My Recollections of Ludwig Schnorr of Carolsfeld.

Mastersingers of Nuremberg, The (Die Meistersinger von Nürnberg). Comic opera in three acts.

CHARACTERS

Hans Sachs, Cobbler - - -	Bass
Veit Pogner, Goldsmith - -	Bass
Kunz Vogelgesang, Furrier -	Tenor
Conrad Nachtigall, Buckle-maker - - - - - - -	Bass
Sixtus Beckmesser, T o w n Clerk - - - - - - -	Bass
Fritz Kothner, Baker - - -	Bass
Balthazar Zorn, Pewterer - -	Tenor
Ulrich Eislinger, Grocer - -	Tenor
August Moser, Tailor - - -	Tenor
Hermann O r t e l, S o a p-boiler - - - - - -	Bass
Hans Schwarz, S t o c k i n g-weaver - - - - - -	Bass
Hans Folz, Coppersmith - -	Bass
Walther (or Walter) von Stolzing, a young Franconian knight - - - - -	Tenor
David, apprentice to Hans Sachs - - - - - - -	Tenor
A night watchman - - - -	Bass
Eva, daughter of Pogner - -	Soprano
Magdalena, Eva's nurse - -	Mezzo-soprano

TIME—Middle of 16th century

PLACE—Nuremberg.

First drafts made in Marienbad summer of 1844 and presented to Frau Mathilde Wesendonck. Book completed in Paris in the winter of 1861-62. Music composed in Biebrich, a small town opposite Mainz, at Penzing, near Vienna, and finished at Triebschen Oct. 24, 1867. Copyright sold to Messrs. Schott, of Mainz. Pianoforte arrangement by Tausig published in 1867. Full score published 1868.

MEI

SOURCES

Wagenseil's *Nürnberger Chronik* (1697); also works of Hans Sachs, a cobbler and poet, and E. T. A. Hoffmann's tale *Meister Martin der Küfer von Nürnberg und seine Gesellen,* as well as Hoffmann's story about a legendary contest at Wartburg contained in his *Serapions Brüder,* Vol. II.

The overture was first performed in November, 1862, conducted by Wagner, at a concert given by Wendelin Weissheimer in the Gewandhaus at Leipzig.

Opera first produced at the Royal Court Theatre, Munich, on June 21, 1868, with von Bülow as conductor, and Hans Richter as chorus-master.

ORIGINAL CAST

Hans Sachs	Betz
Veit Pogner	Bausewein
Kunz Vogelgesang	Heinrich
Conrad Nachtigall	Sigl
Sixtus Beckmesser	Hölzel
Fritz Kothner	Fischer
Balthazar Zorn	Weixlstorfer
Ulrich Eislinger	Hoppe
Augustin Moser	Pöppl
Hermann Ortel	Thoms
Hans Schwarz	Graffer
Hans Folz	Hayn
Walther von Stolzing	Nachbauer
David	Schlosser
Eva	Fräulein Mallinger
Magdalena	Frau Diez
Ein Nachtwächter	Lang

First performed in America at the Metropolitan Opera House, New York, Jan. 4, 1886.

75

MEI

Hans Sachs - - - - -	Emil Fischer
Veit Pogner - - - - -	Joseph Staudigl
Kunz Vogelgesang - -	Herr Dworsky
Conrad Nachtigall - - -	Emil Sänger
Sixtus Beckmesser - -	Otto Kemlitz
Fritz Kothner - - - -	Herr Lehmler
Balthazar Zorn - - - -	Herr Hoppe
Ulrich Eislinger - - -	Herr Klaus
Augustin Moser - - -	Herr Langer
Hermann Ortel - - -	Herr Dörfler
Hans Schwarz - - - -	Herr Eissbeck
Hans Folz - - - - -	Herr Anlauf
Walther von Stolzing - -	Albert Stritt
David - - - - - - -	Herr Krämer
Eva - - - - - - -	Auguste Krauss (Mrs. Seidl)
Magdalena - - - - -	Marianne Brandt
Nachtwächter - - - -	Carl Kauffmann

CONDUCTOR: Anton Seidl

THE OPERA

Argument

Act I

At the close of a service in St. Catherine's Church a young Franconian knight, Walther von Stolzing, meets Eva, rich goldsmith Veit Pogner's daughter, and confesses his love for her. Pogner is greatly disturbed because of the low estimation in which the burghers are held, due to absorption in business. So he offers his daughter, with all his money, to the winner in a contest of song of the Mastersingers on Midsummer Day. Walther decides to join their guild and become a competitor. David, an apprentice, instructs him in the pedantic rules for singing prescribed by the guild. At

76

his request Walther is examined and Beckmesser, a man of middle age and town clerk, his rival for Eva's hand, is chosen as critic or marker, much to the town clerk's disgust. Before Walther's song is finished Beckmesser shows his blackboard covered with marks and although championed by the shoemaker-poet, Hans Sachs, Walther is rejected.

Act II

In a street before Hans Sachs' house. On hearing of Walther's rejection Eva decides to elope with him, but the watchman appearing they hide. Beckmesser then comes, playing his lute, to serenade Eva. Hans Sachs moves his bench to the street, hammers away at a shoe and sings humorous songs repeatedly interrupting the serenade. David appears and thinking the serenade is intended for Magdalena, who is disguised at a window, beats Beckmesser. The noise arouses all the neighbors who join in the tumult until dispersed by sound of the watchman's horn.

Act III

Walther, who had spent the night with Hans Sachs on account of the interrupted elopement, tells Sachs of a dream he had, in which occurred the melody of a wonderful song—the prize-song. Sachs records it on paper and they leave. Beckmesser enters and steals the song, supposing it has been composed by Sachs and hopes thereby to win the prize. At the public festival Beckmesser sings but becomes confused and his song is drowned by laughter. Sachs proposes that the prize shall be awarded to anyone, even though not a member of the guild, who can sing that song properly and it is agreed to. Walther comes forward, sings the song, and wins Eva for his bride.

Ernest Newman says this is the greatest of all comedies in music, "if indeed 'comedy' is the correct word to apply to an opera that, in addition to its humorous episodes, contains so much that is the quintessence of serious beauty, of profound philosophy, and of mellow wisdom." [1]

For Leading Motives see the appendix, p. 187.

Melot. A character in *Tristan and Isolde*; baritone. A courtier. Act 2, scene 3; Act 3, scenes 3, 4. Rôle created by Heinrich.

Mensch und die bestehende Gesellschaft, Der. See Man and Established Society.

Messenger of Peace, A. A character in *Rienzi*; soprano. Act 2, No. 5. Rôle created by Thiele.

Meudon. Suburb of Paris. Residence of Richard Wagner Apr. 29 to Oct. 30, 1841. Here *The Flying Dutchman* was composed in 1841.

Meyerbeer, Giacomo. Dramatic composer. Born Sept. 5, 1791, at Berlin of Jewish parents, son of a wealthy Berlin banker. Mother, Amalie (Wulf). Composer of *Robert le Diable, Les Huguenots, Le Prophète* and *L'Africaine*. To him Wagner journeyed for encouragement and help in getting his work introduced. They met at Boulogne and Meyerbeer praised his libretto and the completed first two acts of *Rienzi*. Died May 2, 1864.

Mignonne. Listed in Musical Works. Words by Ronsard. Published in *Gazette Musicale*. Written in Paris in the period of 1839-40. Appeared as a musical supplement to Lewald's *Europa*, 1841 and 1842. Republished with a German translation 1871.

---

[1] *Stories of the Great Operas*, p.62. Garden City Pub. Co. Inc. Garden City, N.Y. 1928-30.

Mime. A character in *The Ring*; tenor. A Nibelung, brother of Alberich.
Das Rheingold, Scene 3. Rôle created by Carl Schlosser.
Siegfried, Acts 1, 2. Rôle created by Carl Schlosser.
Wagner, it is supposed, found this name in the Thidrek Saga, in which Mimir is a crafty smith, brother of Regin. Regin, according to this Saga, is the name of the dragon. A child comes to Mimir in the woods and he rears it and calls it Siegfried.

Mitterwürzer. Created the part of Wolfram in *Tannhäuser.*

Mittheilung an den Redaktem der "Neuen Zeitschrift für Musik", Eine. See Gluck's Overture to Iphigenia in Aulis.

Mittheilung an meine Freunde, Eine. See Communication to my friends, A.

Modern. P.W. 6. Published in *Bayreuther Blätter* March 1878.

Möller, Abraham. A Königsberg friend who aided Wagner in escaping from Riga.

Monsalvat. A wild region placed by the composer in Northern Spain as the location of the Temple which housed the Holy Grail. Scene of Act 1 of *Parsifal.*

Morelli, ——. A baritone; sang rôle of Wolfram in *Tannhäuser* in Paris, March 13, 1861.

Morgenlich leuchtend in rosigem Schein. Walther's Prize Song in *Die Meistersinger*, Act 3.

Morold. Brother-in-law of King Gurmun, in *Tristan.*

Moser, August. One of the mastersingers in *Die Meistersinger*; tenor. A tailor. Acts 1, 3. Rôle created by Pöppl.

Motives. See Leading Motives, also appendix p. 187.

Mozart. Listed in Musical Works. An arrangement of *Don Juan*. Revised dialogue and recitatives. Performed at Zürich 1850. Unpublished.

Müller, Alexander. Musician. Friend in Zürich of Wagner. Born 1808 in Erfurt. Pupil of Hummel and Andre in Offenbach. Came to Zürich in 1834; founded the Müller Choral Society, a mixed chorus, 1842-49, presenting oratorios. From time to time was conductor at the stock theatre. He was presented with citizenship by the city of Zürich. Died Jan. 28, 1863 in that city.

Müller, Gottlieb. Music teacher at Leipzig. Engaged as teacher for Richard Wagner. Afterward organist at Altenburg.

Munich. First complete performance of *Die Feen* on Jan. 29, 1888. Here also were first produced *Tristan and Isolde* (June 10, 1865), *Die Meistersinger* (June 21, 1868), *Das Rheingold* (Sept. 22, 1869), and *Die Walküre* (June 26, 1870). King Ludwig first heard Wagner's works in this city.

Museum, Richard Wagner Memorial. See Bayreuth.

Music of the Future. P.W. 4. A letter to a French friend, Fr. Villot, as preface to a prose translation, in French, of Wagner's opera-poems, i.e., *The Flying Dutchman, Tannhäuser, Lohengrin*, and *Tristan and Isolde*. Published by J. J. Weber, Leipzig, 1861.

Musical Criticism, On. P.W. 3. A letter to the Editor of the *Neue Zeitschrift für Musik.* It appeared in that periodical Feb. 6, 1852.

Musical Works. Other than operas and music-dramas.

ORCHESTRAL AND CHORAL WORKS

At Weber's Grave
A Faust Overture
Great Festival March
Greeting to the King, 1844
Incidental music (songs) to a fairy farce by Gleich
Kaiser March
The Love Feast of the Apostles
March of Allegiance
New Year's Cantata
Overture in B
Overture in C
Overture in D minor
Overture "Polonie" (Polonia) C major
Overture "Rule Britannia"
Overture "Columbus"
Siegfried Idyll
Special Cantata
Symphony in C major

PIANOFORTE PIECES

Album-leaf for Frau Betty Schott, in E ♭
An Album-leaf for Fürstin Metternich, in C
Album-Sonata for Frau Mathilde Wesendonck, in E ♭
Fantasie F ♯ minor
Polonaise, D (Opus 2)
Sonata, B ♭ (Opus 1)

SONGS

Carnival Song from *Das Liebesverbot,* 1835-36
Five Poems:
  1. The Angel (Der Engel)

81

MUS-NIB

2. Stand Still (Stehe still)
3. In the Greenhouse (Im Treibhaus)
4. Sorrows (Schmerzen)
5. Dreams (Träume)

Sleep, My Child (Dors, mon enfant)
Mignonne (Mignonne)
Waiting (L'Attente)
Kraft-Song of Strength (Kraft-Liedchen)
The Fir-tree (Der Tannenbaum)
The Two Grenadiers (Les deux Grenadiers)

ARRANGEMENTS, ETC.

Allegro to the aria of Aubrey in the *Vampire*, by Marschner
Beethoven—Ninth Symphony
Donizetti—Elisir d'Amore
Donizetti—La Favorite
Gluck—Iphigénie en Aulide
Halévy—La Reine de Chypre
Halévy—Le Guittarero
Mozart—Don Juan
Palestrina—Stabat Mater

Music-dramas. This term was not used earlier than 1851, and applies to compositions subsequent to that period. *Lohengrin* and its predecessors were termed "operas" by Wagner.

Music-School for Munich, A. P.W. 4. Report to His Majesty King Ludwig II of Bavaria upon a German Music-School to be founded in Munich. Written in March 1865. Plan rejected as too expensive by a commission appointed to consider its feasibility, composed of Intendant von Perfall, Franz Lachner, W. H. Riehl, Hans von Bülow and Richard

Wagner. An institute, modified after this plan, was erected in Munich with von Bülow at its head.

Musikalische Kritik, Über. See Musical Criticism, On.

My Recollections of Ludwig Schnorr of Carolsfeld. P.W. 4. Written at Lucèrne, May 5, 1868. Published in *Neue Zeitschrift für Musik* June 5, 12, 1868.

N

Nachruf an L. Spohr und Chordirector W. Fischer. See Homage to Ludwig Spohr and Chorus-Master Wilhelm Fischer.

Nachtigall, Conrad. One of the mastersingers in *Die Meistersinger*; bass. A bucklemaker. Acts 1, 3. Rôle created by Sigl.

Naples. The home of Richard Wagner was the Villa D'Angri.

Neidhöhle. The Cave of Envy. To this place Fafner retired after slaying Fasolt—in *Das Rheingold*—where he changed by power of the Tarnhelm into a dragon in order to guard his treasure.

Neiding. A character in *Wieland the Smith.* King of the Niaren.

New Year's Cantata. Listed in Musical Works. Introduction and two choral pieces. Unpublished. Performed at Magdeburg on New Year's Eve 1834-35 and at Bayreuth May 22, 1873.

Nibelheim. The realm of the Nibelungs, characters in *The Ring.*

Nibelung. A gnome. See *Ring of the Nibelungs, The.*

Nibelung Myth as Sketch for a Drama, The. P.W. 7
Written in the summer of 1848. Issued as a pamphlet by Wigand of Leipzig in 1849.

Nibelungen Lied. Story founded on the Volsunga
Saga. The legend of Siegfried's exploits. See a
complete and scholarly treatise on the great volume
of Nibelungen literature in H. v. Wolzogen's *Der
Nibelungenmythos in Sage und Litteratur.* Weber,
Berlin, 1876.

Niemann, Albert. Distinguished Prussian operatic
tenor. Born Jan. 15, 1831 at Erxleben, Magdeburg,
the son of a hotel-keeper. Studied singing under
Nusch, a baritone, F. Schneider and Duprez. Sang
at Dessau in chorus and minor parts. In 1860 was
engaged at the Hanover Opera and in 1866-89 at
the Berlin Opera and elsewhere. Selected by Wagner
for the title role in *Tannhäuser* at the Paris Académie
March 13, 1861, and for the part of Siegmund in the
trilogy at Bayreuth in 1876. He united great vocal
warmth and declamatory power with fine impressive
acting. Married, first (in 1859), Marie Seebach,
and, second, Redwig Raabe (in 1870). Came to
America in 1886 and 1887, where he sang in German
in New York with great success. Retired in 1887.
Died at Berlin Jan. 13, 1917.

Night Watchman. A character in *Die Meistersinger*;
bass. Act 2. Rôle created by Lang.

Nornir. Characters in *The Ring*; contralto, mezzo-
soprano and soprano Fates, representing Past,
Present and Future.

Götterdämmerung, Prelude. Rôles created by
Johanna Jachmann-Wagner, Josephine Scheffsky,
Fredericke Grün.

Nothung. "Needful." The sword forged by Siegfried in the first act of *Siegfried.* Otherwise called "Balmung."

Notices. P.W. 4.
1. W. H. Riehl.
2. Ferdinand Hiller.
   1 and 2 published in *Süddeutsche Presse*, 1867, and in Vol. 8 of *Gesammelte Schriften* (Collected Writings).
3. A Remembrance of Rossini.
   Published in Augsburg *Allegemeine Zeitung* Dec. 17, 1868, dated Triebschen, near Lucerne, Dec. 7, 1868.
4. Eduard Devrient.
   Published in 1869, as a pamphlet entitled "Herr E. Devrient und sein Styl" under the pseudonym of "Wilhelm Drach."

Nureddin. A character in *The Saracen Woman*; tenor.

O

O Night of Love! (O sink' hernieder Nacht der Liebe) Duet between Tristan and Isolde, Act 2, scene 2.

Of what use is this knowledge? See Religion and Art, No. 1.

Offenes Schreiben an Herrn Ernst' von Weber, verfasser der Schrift: "Die Folterkammern der Wissenschaft." See Vivisection, On.

Offenes Schreiben an Herrn Friedrich Schön in Worms. See Stipendiary Fund, The.

Ofterdingen, Heinrich von. A celebrated German poet of the thirteenth century. Wagner created the character of Tannhäuser out of this poet and a mythical figure actually named Tannhäuser.

Ollivier, Emile. Born at Marseilles 1825. Died 1913. French statesman and husband of Liszt's daughter Blandine. Friend and visitor of Wagner in Paris.

Oper und Drama. See Opera and Drama.

Opera and Drama. P.W. 2.
1. Opera and the Nature of Music.
2. The Play and the Nature of Dramatic Poetry.
3. The Arts of Poetry and Tone in the Drama of the Future.

Published in the *Deutsche Monatsschrift.* Book published by J. J. Weber, Leipzig, 1851. Cites principles which should govern the creation of art-work for the stage.

Opera and the Nature of Music. See Opera and Drama, Part 1.

Opera Poetry and Composition in Particular, On. P.W. 6. Published in the *Bayreuther Blätter* Sept. 1879.

Opernaufführung in Leipzig, Über eine. See Spohr's "Jessonda" at Leipzig.

Opern-Dichten und Komponiren im Besonderen, Über das. See Opera Poetry and Composition in Particular, On.

Orchestral Works. See Musical Works.

Orsini, Paolo. A character in *Rienzi*; bass. A patrician. Act 1, No. 1; Act 2, Nos. 6, 7. Rôle created by Wächter.

Ortel, Hermann. One of the mastersingers in *Die Meistersinger*; bass. A soap-boiler. Acts 1, 3. Rôle created by Thoms.

Ortlinde. A character in *The Ring*; soprano of dramatic quality. A valkyrie.
Die Walküre, Act 3. Rôle created at first Festspielhaus performance by Marie Lehmann.

Ortrud. A character in *Lohengrin*; mezzo-soprano. Wife of Frederick of Telramund, Count of Brabant. Act 1, scene 3; Act 2, scenes 1, 2, 4, 5; Act 3, scene 3. Daughter of Radbod, Prince of Friesland. Rôle created by Fräulein Fastlinger.

Ouverture, Über die. See Overture, On the.

Overture, On the. P.W. 7. Published in *Gazette Musicale* Jan. 10, 14, 17, 1841. Reprinted in his *Collected Writings* 1871.

Overture in B ♭. Listed in Musical Works. Kettledrum overture. Unpublished. Score is lost. Performed 1830 at Leipzig under the direction of Heinrich Dorn.

Overture in C (Konzert-Ouverture-Ziemlich fugirt). Listed in Musical Works. Concert overture—somewhat in the style of a fugue. Unpublished. Written 1831. Performed for first time Apr. 30, 1833 at an Euterpe concert at Leipzig, then at the Gewandhaus. Also on May 22, 1873 at Bayreuth.

Overture, D minor. Listed in Musical Works. Composed 1831. Unpublished. Performed Dec. 25, 1831 at Gewandhaus, Leipzig. Score at Bayreuth.

Overture to Der Fliegende Holländer (The Flying Dutchman). See Explanatory Programmes, No. 3.

Overture to Tannhäuser. See Explanatory Programmes, No. 4.

P

Pätz, Johanna Rosine. (Sept. 19, 1774-Jan. 9, 1848) Wife of Carl Friedrich Wagner; mother of Richard Wagner.

Palermo. Wagner completed the *Parsifal* score on Jan. 13, 1882, at the Hotel des Palmes.

Palestrina. Listed in Musical Works. *Stabat Mater.* Arranged with notations indicating style of execution, 1848. Score published 1877.

Paris. Wagner lived at No. 23 Rue de la Tonnellerie in the old Quartier des Halles, since demolished. In its place is No. 31 Rue du Pont-neuf. It is decorated with a memorial tablet. Then he lived on the fourth floor of 25 Rue du Helder, off the Boulevard des Italiens. Also at Rue Jacob No. 14.

He removed to Meudon, a suburb, Apr. 29, 1841, residing at No. 3 Avenue de Meudon. Thence back to Paris at No. 10 Rue Jacob. He left Paris on Thursday, Apr. 7, 1842 for Dresden; returned Feb. 1, 1850 and dwelt at 59 Rue de Provence. In 1859 he lived in the Rue Newton, afterward at No. 3 Rue d'Aumale.

In Paris or Meudon he wrote the poem and score of *The Flying Dutchman,* first conceived *Tannhäuser* and *Lohengrin,* drafted *Wieland the Smith,* and wrote the text of *Die Meistersinger.*

Parisian Amusements. P.W. 8. Published in Lewald's *Europa* 1841 under the pseudonym of "W. Freudenfeuer." Not included in *Gesammelte Schriften.*

Parisian Fatalities. P.W. 8. Published in Lewald's *Europa* 1841 under the pseudonym of "W. Freudenfeuer." Not included in *Gesammelte Schriften.*

Parsifal. A character in *Parsifal*; tenor. Traditionally, son of a king called Gamuret and father of Lohengrin. Acts 1, 2, 3. Rôle created by Winkelmann.

Parsifal. A Sacred Stage Festival Play (Bühnenweihfestspiel) in three acts.

CHARACTERS

Amfortas, son of Titurel, ruler of the Kingdom of the Grail - - - - - - - -	Baritone-bass
Titurel, former ruler - - -	Bass
Gurnemanz, a veteran Knight of the Grail - - - - - -	Bass
Klingsor, a magician - - - -	Bass
Parsifal - - - - - - - - -	Tenor
Kundry - - - - - - - - -	Soprano
First and Second Knights - -	Tenor and Bass
Four Esquires - - - - - -	Sopranos and Tenors
Six of Klingsor's F l o w e r Maidens - - - - - - -	Sopranos

TIME—The Middle Ages

PLACE—Spain, near and in the Castle of the Holy Grail; in Klingsor's enchanted castle and in the garden of his castle.

First sketches were made at Zürich in 1857 and the first sketch of libretto made in August, 1865. The poem was finished in 1877 at Bayreuth. Sketch of the music was begun at Bayreuth 1877, prelude written in December, 1878 and music completed April 26, 1879.

Score completed Jan. 13, 1882 at Palermo. Pianoforte score published 1882; full score 1884. Pianoforte arrangement by Josef Rubenstein.

Wagner read the poem on May 17, 1877 to friends at the home of Edward Dannreuther in London, and to German friends at Heidelberg on July 8. It was published in December 1877.

The Prelude was performed for the first time at the Wahnfried Christmas festival of 1878 by the Neiningen Court Orchestra under Wagner in celebration of his wife's birthday. Wagner wrote for King Ludwig, in connection with a performance of the Prelude at Munich in 1880, an explanatory note (translated by William Ashton Ellis) :

"LOVE—FAITH :—HOPE?"

FIRST THEME: "LOVE"

"Take ye My body, take My Blood, in token of our love !"
(Repeated in faint whispers by angel-voices)
"Take ye My blood, My body take, in memory of Me !"
(Again repeated in whispers)

SECOND THEME: "FAITH"

"Promise of redemption through faith. Firmly and stoutly faith declares itself, exalted, willing even in suffering. To the promise renewed Faith answers from the dimmest heights—as on the pinions of the snow-white dove—hovering downwards—usurping more and more the hearts of men, filling the world, the whole world of Nature, with the mightiest force, then glancing up again to heaven's vault as if appeased.

"But once more, from out the awe of solitude, throbs forth the cry of loving pity; the agony, the holy sweat of Olivet, the divine death-throes of Golgotha—the body pales, the blood flows forth, and glows now in the chalice with the heavenly glow of blessing shedding on all that lives and languishes the grace of ransom won by Love. For him who—fearful rue for sin at heart—must quail before the godlike vision of the Grail, for Amfortas, sinful keeper of the halidom, we are made ready: will redemption heal the gnawing torments of his soul? Once more we hear the promise, and—we hope !"

First performance of *Parsifal* at Bayreuth on July 26, 1882, Levi conductor.

ORIGINAL CAST

Parsifal - - - - - - - Winkelmann
Amfortas - - - - - - - Reichmann

Titurel	- - - - - - -	Kindermann
Klingsor	- - - - - - -	Hill
Gurnemanz	- - - - - -	Scaria
Kundry	- - - - - - -	Materna

The copyright expired at the end of 1913 and early the following year it was performed in various European cities. The first performance in America was a concert version by the Oratorio Society of New York, Walter Damrosch conductor, on March 3, 1886.

SOURCES

First suggestions for an opera on this subject came to Wagner in 1848, in his *Jesus of Nazareth*. The story of Parsifal came to his attention in 1854 while at work on *Die Walküre*. He derived the word "Parsifal" from the Arabic "Parsi Fal," the pure fool. In Cornish language "par" means fellow and "full" simple-minded. The *Parzival* of Wolfram von Eschenbach published in 1477, was the immediate source.

"Now the Grail, after my reading, is the cup of the Last Supper, wherein Joseph of Arimathea gathered the blood of the Saviour on the cross."
From a letter of Richard Wagner to Mathilde Wesendonck, May 30, 1859, translated by W. Ashton Ellis.

Parsifal, son of Gamuret, is the father of Lohengrin, who dwells in the Grailburg, in the neighborhood of Castle Monsalvat, in Spain. Thematic treatises on the *Parsifal* score have been prepared by Wolzogen, Heinz, Eichberg and Kobbé; also by Kufferath, who has written a very complete and valuable treatise dealing with the legendary sources, the poem, and the music from different viewpoints. A splendid account for lay readers is by Charles Dudley Warner in the *Atlantic Monthly*, January 1883.

91

Legendary

Foreword

The story deals with a legend of the Holy Grail. It located Monsalvat, a castle of the Grail, on a mountain in Spain. Here, the holy knights guard the spear with which Christ's side was pierced and the cup from which He drank at the Last Supper and into which was received His blood while on the cross. Only the pure in heart may be of this chosen company. Miraculous powers are conferred upon them by the Grail. Titurel had been given the care of the Grail by the angels but upon growing old he entrusted it to his son, Amfortas. Klingsor, the great Enemy of Good, lured Amfortas into his flower garden inhabited by beautiful maidens. Although Amfortas was armed with the blessed spear he succumbed to the allurements of Kundry, a strange person, who had the power to change herself into different forms. Having yielded to his passion, he lost his power and was wounded by Klingsor with the blessed spear. Since then the wound has remained open and cannot be healed until a saver or redeemer comes and with the point of the blessed spear causes it to heal. The saver will come in the person of a guileless Fool, being absolutely pure and ignorant of evil.

The Music-Drama

Argument

Act I

At the beginning of the play Amfortas is on his way to his daily bath which he takes vainly for relief from the agony of the wound. Kundry brings him balsam from Arabia but he hopes nothing until the advent of the "fool." Gurnemanz, a knight of the Grail, tells the followers of Amfortas how he received the wound. At this time Parsifal, an untutored youth, son of Herzeleide and King Gamuret, appears. Because of his simplicity, fearlessness and absolute unconciousness of evil, Gurnemanz suspects that this youth is the guileless Fool and invites him to the Temple of the Grail where the knights are to hold their mystic Love-Feast. Amfortas is borne in to the Love-Feast on a litter preceded by youths carrying a veiled shrine. Titurel orders Amfortas to unveil the Holy Grail; he refuses until he is reminded of the promised redemption. He then obeys and the cup is uncovered. However, Amfortas does not join in the Love Feast or Lord's Supper, nor does Parsifal. After the Grail is borne out, Gurnemanz tries to question Parsifal but without desired results.

Act II

Klingsor realizes too that Parsifal is the guileless Fool and as such is a menace to him. Therefore he awakens Kundry and demands of her that she use all her power to seduce Parsifal as she did Amfortas. She tempts him as best she can but all her allurements fail. Parsifal flings himself on his knees and prays. Kundry then knows he is proof and will not yield to temptation. She calls Klingsor who appears brandishing the blessed spear and hurls it at Parsifal. The spear halts in midair, the guileless Fool grasps it and with it makes the sign of the cross. Klingsor is annihilated and the castle crumbles into dust. Kundry falls senseless.

Act III

Parsifal wanders about the world for years guarding but never wielding the holy spear. Finally, on Good Friday, Gurnemanz beholds a knight in black armor, carrying a long spear, wending his way toward his hut on the border of Monsalvat. He makes no answer to the greetings of Gurnemanz but thrusts his spear into the ground and kneels in prayer. Finally he relates the adventures through which he has passed in his wanderings. Gurnemanz welcomes him as the Messenger who is to heal Amfortas and restore to the Knights Templars the mysterious blessings of the Holy Grail, the lack of which has caused Titurel to perish.

The body of Titurel is carried into the Temple of the Holy Grail. Amfortas also comes, preceded by the veiled shrine, while the knights solemnly intone a song in honor of the sacred cup and in remembrance of Titurel. They cry to Amfortas to unveil the cup but he refuses. At this point Parsifal appears and with the blessed spear quietly touches Amfortas' still gaping wound. At this healing touch Parsifal, who is now king, commands the Grail bearers to unveil the shrine. The consummation of the mission entrusted to Parsifal is proclaimed.

See *Bayreuther Blätter.* For Leading Motives see the appendix, p. 187.

Parsifal at Bayreuth, 1882. P.W. 6. Published in *Bayreuther Blätter* Nov., Dec. 1882.

Pasticcio. P.W. 8. "Pasticcio" means a pasty. Published in Schumann's *Neue Zeitschrift* Nov. 6, 10, 1834. Wagner signed the article "Canto Spianato." Not included in *Gesammelte Schriften.*

Peps. Name of Wagner's dog, of whom he was inordinately fond. He always asserted humorously that Peps had helped him compose *Tannhäuser* by answering in barks to questions as to whether he liked certain parts or not.

Performing of "Tannhäuser," On the. P.W. 3. A treatise by Richard Wagner of which 200 copies were printed and distributed among all the German opera houses. In this he gave minute directions to singers and stage directors. Portions of this article were published in the *Neue Zeitschrift* Dec. 3, 24, 1852, Jan. 1, 7, 14, 1853.

Pergolesi's "Stabat Mater." See German Musician in Paris, A. No. 4a.

Pianoforte Pieces. See Musical Works.

Pilgerfahrt zu Beethoven, Eine. See German Musician in Paris, A. No. 1: A Pilgrimage to Beethoven.

Pilgrimage to Beethoven, A. See German Musician in Paris, A. No. 1.

Pilgrim's Chorus. *Tannhäuser*, Act 1, scene 3; Act 2, scene 4; Act 3, scene 1.

Plan of Organization of a German National Theatre for the Kingdom of Saxony. P.W. 7. Addressed to the Minister of the Interior. In the Collected Writings Wagner gives the date as 1849, but Ellis shows it to be 1848.

Planer, Christine Wilhelmine (called "Minna"). Actress, friend of Wagner in Magdeburg, to whom he was married on Nov. 24, 1836 in the Tragheimer Church at Königsberg, having become engaged to her while at Magdeburg. His own opinion of the marriage is given in a poem written in his diary on Aug. 4, 1841, in Paris. This may be found in Kürschner's *Wagner Jahrbuch* for 1886, p.290.

Born Sept. 5, 1809, daughter of a Dresden spindle-maker, (Ellis gives the year as 1814), at Öderan, a village between Freiberg and Chemnitz, about half-way between Dresden and Zwickau. Father, Gotthilf Planer, of Dresden, a mechanician. Mother, Johanna Christine Meyer. A good, gentle, loving woman, devoted to him but utterly unable to understand him or to enter into his artistic ideals and purposes. Praeger described her as "handsome but not strikingly so; of medium height, slim figure. She had

95

a pair of soft gazelle-like eyes which were a faithful
index of a tender heart."

She separated from Wagner in August 1861 and
went to live in Dresden where she died on Jan. 25,
1866 of heart disease. Buried in the Anna Friedhof
in Dresden.

Play and the Nature of Dramatic Poetry, The. See
Opera and Drama, Part 2.

Poems. P.W. 4.
1. Rheingold.
Written in 1868.
2. Upon the completion of *Siegfried*.
Apparently composed for King Ludwig's 25th
birthday, Aug. 25, 1869.
3. August 25, 1870.
In celebration of the King's 26th birthday.

Poetry and Composition, On. P.W. 6. Published
in *Bayreuther Blätter*, July 1879.

Pogner, Veit. One of the mastersingers in *Die Meistersinger*; bass. A goldsmith. Acts 1, 2, 3. Rôle created
by Bausewein.

Pollert, Frau. Prima donna, friend of Wagner in
Magdeburg. She played "Isabella" in the only performance of *Das Liebesverbot*.

Polonaise, D. (Opus 2) Listed in Musical Works.
For four hands. Written 1831; published 1832 by
Breitkopf & Härtel.

Polonia. Listed in Musical Works. An overture in
C major. Written 1832 at Leipzig. Published 1904.
Score at Bayreuth. Lost for forty years but found
in 1881 in possession of M. Pasdeloup, Paris conductor, from whom Wagner recovered it. It was
played in that year at Palermo in honor of his wife's
birthday.

Praeger, Ferdinand Christian Wilhelm. Son of Heinrich Aloys Praeger, a violinist, composer, and capellmeister. Born at Leipzig Jan. 22, 1815. Played the cello and piano. Was a teacher of music at the Hague at 16. In 1834 went to London where he settled as a teacher.

Friend and admirer of Wagner. Claimed to have caused his appointment as conductor of the old London Philharmonic but this is disputed by Ellis.

Correspondent of the *Neue Zeitschrift für Musik.* Author of *Wagner as I Knew Him*, published in 1885 (1892),[1] London, which has been criticized severely by the author of the authorized life of the composer, William Ashton Ellis. Died Sept. 2, 1891.

Prague. Wagner here in 1832 began his career as a composer of operas.

Prakriti. The heroine of a drama entitled *The Victors,* of which Wagner made a sketch bearing date of May 16, 1856.

Prelude to Lohengrin. See Lohengrin.

Prize Song. Walther's air in *Die Meistersinger,* Act 3.

Programmatische Erlaüterungen. See Explanatory Programmes.

Prose Sketch for "The Apostle's Love Feast." P.W. 8. Manuscript appeared first, according to Glasenapp, at an auction in Dec. 1886 and then was lost. Later discovered in 1898 at The Royal Library in Berlin and printed in *Bayreuther Blätter* Jan. 1899. Prose sketch of libretto is dated Apr. 21, 1843. Finished sketch, set to music, was performed in the Dresden Frauenkirche on July 6 or 7, 1843. See Love Feast of the Apostles, The.

[1] Longmans, Green & Co., New York.

PRO

Prose Works.

The references to Volumes are to the authorized English translation by William Ashton Ellis. (London: Kegan Paul, Trench, Trubner & Co., 1892-99)
For data see notes under the separate titles elsewhere in this volume.

Actors and Singers. P.W. 5.
Art and Climate. P.W. 1.
Art and Revolution, with Introduction. P.W. 1.
Artist and Critic. P.W. 8.
The Art-Work of the Future. P.W. 1.
Author's Introduction to Vol. II of the *Gesammelte Schriften*. P.W. 7.
Autobiographic Sketch. P.W. 1.

Bayreuth. P.W. 5.
Bayreuth. *Bayreuther Blätter*. P.W. 6.
Beethoven. P.W. 5.
Beethoven's Choral Symphony at Dresden, 1846, together with a program. P.W. 7.
Bellini: A word in season. P.W. 8.

A Capitulation. P.W. 5.
A Communication to My Friends. P.W. 1.

The Destiny of Opera. P.W. 5.

End of the Patronat-Verein. P.W. 6.
Epilogue to the "Nibelung's Ring." P.W. 4.
Explanatory Programmes. P.W. 3.

Der Freischütz in Paris. P.W. 7.

German Art and German Policy. P.W. 4.
A German Musician in Paris. Tales and Articles. P.W. 7.
    1.   A Pilgrimage to Beethoven.
    2.   An End in Paris.
    3.   A Happy Evening.
    4.   On German Music.
    4a.   Pergolesi's *Stabat Mater*.
    5.   The Virtuoso and the Artist.

6.   The Artist and Publicity.
7.   Rossini's *Stabat Mater.*

Gluck's Overture to *Iphigenia in Aulis.*   P.W. 3.
Greeting from Saxony to the Viennese.   Poem.
   P.W. 8.

Halévy and *La Reine de Chypre.*   P.W. 8.
Halévy's *Reine de Chypre.*   P.W. 7.
Homage to Ludwig Spohr and Chorus-Master Wil-
   helm Fischer.   P.W. 3.
The Human Womanly.   As Conclusion of Religion
   and Art.   P.W. 6.

Invitation to the Production of *Tristan* in Munich.
   P.W. 8.

Jesus of Nazareth.   P.W. 8.
Jottings on the Ninth Symphony.   P.W. 8.
Judaism in Music.   P.W. 3.

Letter to H. v. Stein.   P.W. 6.
A letter to Hector Berlioz.   P.W. 4.
Letters and Minor Essays.   P.W. 5.
Letters from Paris, 1841.   P.W. 8.
Das Liebesverbot.   P.W. 7.

Man and Established Society.   P.W. 8.
Mementoes of Spontini.   P.W. 3.
Modern.   P.W. 6.
Music of the Future.   P.W. 4.
A Music-School for Munich.   P.W. 4.
My Recollections of Ludwig Schnorr of Carolsfeld.
   P.W. 4.

The Nibelungen Myth.   A Sketch for a Drama.
   P.W. 7.
Notices.   P.W. 4.
   1. W. H. Riehl.
   2. Ferdinand Hiller.

3. A Remembrance of Rossini.
4. Eduard Devrient.

On Conducting. P.W. 4.
On E. Devrient's *History of German Acting*. P.W. 8.
On Franz Liszt's *Symphonic Poems*. P.W. 3.
On German Opera. P.W. 8.
On Musical Criticism. P.W. 3.
On Opera Poetry and Composition in Particular. P.W. 6.
On Poetry and Composition. P.W. 6.
On State and Religion. P.W. 4.
On Vivisection. P.W. 6.
On the Application of Music to the Drama. P.W. 6.
On Goethe Institute. P.W. 3.
On the Performing of *Tannhäuser*. P.W. 3.
On the Overture. P.W. 7.
Opera and Drama. P.W. 2.

Parisian Amusements. P.W. 8.
Parisian Fatalities. P.W. 8.
Parsifal at Bayreuth, 1882. P.W. 6.
Pasticcio. P.W. 8.
Plan of Organization of a German National Theatre for the Kingdom of Saxony. P.W. 7.
Poems. P.W. 4.
1. *Rheingold*.
2. Upon the completion of *Siegfried*.
3. August 25, 1870.
Prose Sketch for *The Apostles Love Feast*. P.W. 8.
Public and Popularity. P.W. 6.
The Public in Time and Space. P.W. 6.

Religion and Art. P.W. 6.
Remarks on Performing the opera *The Flying Dutch-man*. P.W. 3.
Reminiscences of Auber. P.W. 5.

The Rendering of Beethoven's *Ninth Symphony*. P.W. 5.

Report on the home-bringing of the mortal remains of Karl Maria von Weber from London to Dresden. P.W. 7.

A Report on the production of *Tannhäuser* in Paris. P.W. 3.

A Retrospect of the Stage-Festivals of 1876. P.W. 6.

The Revolution. P.W. 8.

The Saracen Woman. (1841-43). P.W. 8.

Shall we hope? P.W. 6.

Siegfried's Death. P.W. 8.

Speech at Weber's last resting place. P.W. 7.

Spohr's *Jessonda* at Leipzig. P.W. 6.

The Stipendiary Fund. Open letter to Herr Friedrich Schön of Worms. P.W. 6.

Sundry Sketches and Fragments. P.W. 8.

A Theatre at Zürich. P.W. 3.

Theatre-Reform. P.W. 8.

Toast on the Tercentenary of the Royal Kapelle at Dresden. P.W. 7.

To the German Army before Paris. A Poem. P.W. 5.

To the Kingly Friend. Poem. P.W. 4.

The Vienna Opera-House. P.W. 3.

What is German? P.W. 4.

The Wibelungen. World-history as told in Saga. P.W. 7.

Wieland the Smith. A Dramatic Sketch. P.W. 1.

A Youthful Symphony. Report on the reperformance of an early work (Symphony in C). P.W. 6.

Public and Popularity. P.W. 6. Published in the *Bayreuther Blätter* April, June and August, 1878.

Public in Time and Space, The. P.W. 6. Published in the *Bayreuther Blätter* October, 1878.

Publikum in Zeit und Raum, Das. See Public in Time and Space, The.

Publikum und Popularität. See Public and Popularity.

R

Raimondo. A character in *Rienzi*; bass. Papal Legate (Cardinal). Act 1, No. 1; Act 4, No. 12. Rôle created by Vestri.

Reigin. Brother of Alberich, otherwise known as Mime.

Reine de Chypre, La. A dramatic work in five acts by Halévy (Dec. 22, 1841), of which Wagner made a piano score.

Reinmar von Zweter. A character in *Tannhäuser*; bass. Act 1, scene 4; Act 3, scene 3. Rôle created by Risse.

Religion and Art. P.W. 6.
Supplementary:
1. What Boots This Knowledge.
2. Know Thyself.
3. Hero-Dom and Christendom.
Published in the *Bayreuther Blätter* October 1880.

Religion und Kunst. See Religion and Art.

Remarks on Performing the Opera "The Flying Dutchman." P.W. 3. Written either in 1852 or 1853.

Rendering of Beethoven's Ninth Symphony, The. P.W. 5. Published in *Musikalisches Wochenblatt*, April 1873.

Report on the Home-bringing of the Mortal Remains of Karl Maria von Weber from London to Dresden. P.W. 7.

Report on the Production of "Tannhäuser" in Paris, A. P.W. 3. Published in supplement to the *Deutsche Allegemeine Zeitung* April 7, 1861.

Report to His Majesty King Ludwig II of Bavaria upon a German Music-School to be founded in Munich. See Music-School for Munich, A.

Retrospect of the Stage-Festivals of 1876, A. P.W. 6. Published in the *Bayreuther Blätter*, December 1878.

Revolution, The. P.W. 8. Published in Röckel's *Volksblätter*, Feb. 10, Apr. 8, 1849. Revolutionary movements in 1848-49, leading to uprising, induced by the influence of the French Revolution of 1848. People demanded of their king a constitution, free press, trial by jury, national armies and representation.

Rheingold, Das. See *Ring of the Nibelungs, The.* p. 107.

Rhinemaidens. Characters in *The Ring*; Woglinde, Wellgunde, and Flosshilde. They guard the treasure of the Rheingold.

Rhinemaidens' Song. *Das Rheingold*, Scene 4.

Ride of the Valkyries (Walkyrs). Introduction to Act 3, *Die Walküre*. In the production of *Die Walküre* at Munich Wagner required that the Valkyries should ride across the stage on live horses, a difficult and impractical thing to do. Recently filmed projection has been made of the ride by the Munich authorities for the better realistic effect of the scene.

Riegelmann, Therese. Daughter of a grave-digger. Described by Wagner as his "first love affair."

Resident of Würzburg. A chorus girl to whom Wagner gave singing lessons.

Riehl, W. H. See Notices, No. 1.

Rienzi, Cola. A character in *Rienzi*; tenor. Roman Tribune and Papal Notary. Act 1, Nos. 1, 2, 4; Act 2, Nos. 5, 7; Act 3, No. 10; Act 4, No. 12; Act 5, Nos. 13, 14, 16. Rôle created by Tichatschek.

Rienzi. Tragic opera in five acts.

CHARACTERS

Cola Rienzi, Roman Tribune and Papal Notary - - - - - - - - - - -	Tenor
Irene, his sister - - - - - - - -	Soprano
Steffano Colonna, a patrician - - -	Bass
Adriano, Colonna's son - - - - -	Mezzo-soprano
Paolo Orsini, a patrician - - - - -	Bass
Raimondo, Papal Legate (Cardinal) -	Bass
Baroncello ⎫ Roman citizens -	Tenor
Cecco del Vecchio ⎬ (Senators) -	Bass
Messenger of Peace - - - - - -	Soprano

TIME—Middle of 14th Century

PLACE—Rome

Begun at Riga July 26, 1838; first two acts finished in 1839 at Riga and Mitau. Music of the third act begun June 6, 1840, completed Aug. 11; fourth act, begun Aug. 14; fifth act completed Nov. 19. Overture completed Oct. 23. Entire score completed in Paris Nov. 19, 1840.

First produced at the Royal Saxon Court Theatre, Dresden, on Oct. 20, 1842, rehearsals beginning in July 1842. Produced, through the influence of Meyerbeer, at Berlin on Oct. 26, 1847.

Score sent to Herr von Lüttichau, General Director
of the Dresden Opera, accompanied by a letter dated
Dec. 4, 1840, pleading for its presentation at the
opera. Also a letter to Friedrich August II, King
of Saxony, begging permission to dedicate his opera
to him. Both letters are printed in Prölss's *Geschichte
des Hoftheatres in Dresden*, p.118 seq. Corrected
score sent to Theodor Krüttner, conductor of the
local band at Dresden. After his death the score
went to the Eger Museum and is now in the Wagner
Museum at Eisenach.

SOURCES

Based on Edward Bulwer-Lytton's novel *Rienzi,
the Last of the Roman Tribunes*; London, 1835. German translation of Georg Nicolaus Bärmann. The
story of the opera is given in broad outline in Finck's
Wagner and His Works.[1]

THE OPERA
Argument

Act I
An attempt to abduct Irene, the most beautiful
girl in Rome, sister of Rienzi, creates enmity between
the followers of Orsini and those of Colonna. She
is saved by Adriano, with whom she is in love. Rienzi
appears and rebukes them for their conduct. The nobles
continue to fight outside the gates of the city. Rienzi
closes the gates and rouses the people to free themselves
from their oppressors.

Act II
The nobles send messengers of peace and are
admitted into the city on agreeing to take the oath of
fealty. They plot Rienzi's assassination but Adriano

[1] C. Scribner's Sons, New York, 1907.

reveals the conspiracy to Rienzi. The plotters are condemned to death but through intercession of Adriano they are pardoned on their oath of submission.

Act III

The nobles again conspire against the Tribune and Rienzi decides to exterminate them despite the plea of Adriano.

Act IV

After the nobles have been put to death in battle Rienzi returns to celebrate his victory by a *Te Deum*, but is excommunicated by the Pope, through jealousy of his power. The people desert Rienzi.

Act V

Besieged by the populace, alone with his sister Irene in the Capitol, the Tribune dies with her while the building burns. Adriano, who has rushed to save Irene, suffers death also.

ORIGINAL CAST

Cola Rienzi	Tichatschek
Irene	Fräulein Wüst
Steffano Colonna	Dettmer
Adriano	Mme. Schröder-Devrient
Paolo Orsini	Wächter
Raimondo	Vestri
Baroncello	Reinhold
Cecco del Vecchio	Risse
A Messenger of Peace	Thiele

First produced in New York at the Academy of Music March 4, 1878 by the Pappenheim-Adams Company.

CAST

Adriano - - - - - - -	Mme. Eugenia Pappenheim
Irene - - - - - - - -	Miss Alexandre Human
Cola Rienzi - - - - - -	Charles Adams
Paolo Orsini - - - - - -	A. Blum
Steffano Colonna - - - -	H. Wiegand
Raimondo - - - - - -	F. Adolphe
A Messenger of Peace - - -	Miss Cooney

CONDUCTOR, Max Maretzek

Riga. Wagner lived here shortly after his marriage to Minna Planer, in a house in the outskirts of the town, the Thau House on the Schmiedestrasse, since demolished. Afterwards, he resided at 9 Alexanderstrasse for the major portion of his stay. The house belonged to Michael Ivan Bodrow, a Russian trader. Here the first two acts of *Rienzi* were composed.

Ring of the Nibelungs, The. A Stage Festival Play for Three Days and one Preliminary Evening, comprising *Das Rheingold, Die Walküre, Siegfried* and *Götterdämmerung.*

The poem, elaborated from *Siegfried's Tod* (Siegfried's Death), q.v., was finished Dec. 31, 1852, with three dramas and a prologue. The text was published as a piece of literature at Vienna. Early in 1853 Wagner had 50 copies printed, sending Liszt a parcel Feb. 11, 1853. Wagner read it for the first time about Christmas, 1852, at Mariafeld, consuming three evenings, as told by Frau Wille. On Feb. 16-19, 1853, it was read at the Hotel Baur, Zürich. Much of the scoring was done in London in 1855.

First performed at Bayreuth on Aug. 13, 14, 16, 17, 1876; New York, at the Metropolitan Opera

107

RING

House, Mar. 4, 5, 8, 11, 1889; without cuts, Jan. 12, 17, 19, 24, 1899.

The poems were written in reverse order but the music was composed in proper order of *Das Rheingold, Die Walküre, Siegfried* and *Götterdämmerung* (Twilight of the Gods). Details of the writing of the poem may be found in correspondence with Liszt, Uhlig, Fischer and Heine, published in 1887-88 by Breitkopf & Härtel. Pianoforte arrangement is by Klindworth.

SOURCES

Norse mythology, the Volsunga Saga, and the *Nibelungen Lied.* For further details as to sources see *The Fall of the Nibelung,* English translation by Margaret Armour; *The Volsunga Saga,*[1] translated by William Morris and E. Magnussen, and William Morris's poem "Sigurd the Volsung."

"The central motive of the drama as Wagner has conceived it is Wotan's love for power. To consolidate his power he has had a great castle, Valhalla, built for him by the giants. For the ultimate payment of the giant's wage he has trusted more or less to luck. When the time arrives for payment it comes about, in ways that will be described in the following analysis, that he has to satisfy them with gold stolen from the Rhinemaidens by Alberich, upon which, when it was taken from him in turn by Wotan, Alberich has laid a curse. From the gold Alberich has had made for himself a ring that confers on its possessor power over the world; and this ring passes into the possession of one of the giants, Fafner.

Wotan's problem, during the three evenings of the Ring, is to ensure that the ring will come into the possession of someone who will not use it, as Alberich would were he to regain possession of it, for the destruction of the gods. The devious ways by which this is brought about are best told by a straightforward account of *The Ring* as it is set upon the stage in four consecutive evenings."

Ernest Newman, in Stories of the Great Operas, p. 160.[2]

[1] The Walter Scott Pub. Co., New York, 1870.
[2] Garden City Pub. Co., Garden City, New York, 1928-30.

See Bayreuth; Epilogue to the Nibelung's Ring; Retrospect of the Stage Festivals of 1876, A. For Leading Motives see the appendix, p. 187.

THE RHINEGOLD

(*Das Rheingold*)

A music-drama; prologue in four scenes to *The Ring of the Nibelungs.*

CHARACTERS

Wotan -		-	Baritone-bass
Donner -	*Gods*	-	Baritone-bass
Froh -		-	Tenor
Loge -		-	Tenor
Fasolt -	*Giants*	-	Baritone-bass
Fafner -		-	Bass
Alberich -	*Nibelungs*	-	Baritone-bass
Mime -		-	Tenor
Fricka -		-	Soprano
Freia -	*Goddesses*	-	Soprano
Erda -		-	Mezzo-soprano
Woglinde		-	Soprano
Wellgunde	*Rhinemaidens*	-	Soprano
Flosshilde		-	Mezzo-soprano

TIME—Legendary

PLACE—Bed of the Rhine; a mountainous district near the Rhine; the subterranean caverns of Nibelheim.

Poem begun at Dresden 1848; finished at Zürich 1851-52. Composition of music begun Nov. 1, 1853 at Spezia; draft finished Jan. 14, 1854; first act and part of second act finished by July, 1857. Scoring begun

RING

Oct. 1853 and finished May 28, 1854. First engraved vocal score (Klindworth's original arrangement) 1861, by Schott & Co. Full score published 1873.

First produced at the Royal Court Theatre in Munich on Sept. 22, 1869, Franz Wüllner conductor.

Original Cast

Wotan	Kindermann
Donner	Heinrich
Froh	Nachbaur
Loge	Vogl
Alberich	Fischer
Mime	Schlosser
Fasolt	Polzer
Fafner	Bausewein
Fricka	Fräulein Stehle
Freia	Fräulein Müller
Erda	Fräulein Seehofer
Woglinde	Fr. Kaufmann
Wellgunde	Frau Vogel
Flosshilde	Fräulein Ritter

First authorized performance, at the Festspielhaus, Bayreuth, Aug. 13, 1876.

Cast

Wotan	Franz Betz
Donner	Eugen Gura
Froh	Georg Unger
Loge	Heinrich Vogel
Alberich	Carl Hill
Mime	Carl Schlosser
Fasolt	Albert Eilers
Fafner	Fritz von Reichenberg
Fricka	Friedericke Grün
Freia	Marie Haupt
Erda	Luise Jäide

Woglinde   - - - -   Lilli Lehmann
Wellgunde   - - - -   Marie Lehmann
Flosshilde - - - -   Marie Lammert

First performed in America at the Metropolitan
Opera House, New York, Jan. 4, 1889.

CAST

Wotan   - - - - -   Emil Fischer
Donner   - - - - -   Alois Grienauer
Froh   - - - - - - Albert Mittelhauser
Loge   - - - - - - Max Alvary
Alberich - - - - -   Joseph Beck
Mime   - - - - - - Wilhelm Sedlmayer
Fasolt   - - - - - - Ludwig Mödlinger
Fafner   - - - - -   Eugen Weiss
Fricka   - - - - -   Fanny Moran-Olden
Freia   - - - - - - Katti Bettaque
Erda   - - - - - - Hedwig Reil
Woglinde - - - -   Sophie Traubmann
Wellgunde - - - -   Felici Koschoska
Flosshilde - - - -   Hedwig Reil

CONDUCTOR, Anton Seidl

THE MUSIC-DRAMA
Argument

Scene I

Alberich, a Nibelung, visits the Rhinemaidens
Woglinde, Wellgunde and Flosshilde, who are guarding
the mysterious treasure of the Rhinegold. Goaded to
frenzy by their contempt and mockery he renounces
love forever and so is able to lay hold of the Rhinegold and make from it a Ring which confers upon its
possessor mighty power.

111

Scene II

Wotan, chief of the gods, possesses a strong love
for power. To show his supremacy he has had a great
castle, Valhalla, built for him by the giants Fasolt and
Fafner, and at the instigation of Loge, the god of fire,
agreed to remunerate them by yielding Freia, the goddess of youth and beauty. Wotan tries to avoid carrying out the bargain and the giants offer to take instead
the gold which Alberich had stolen in payment for their
work. Wotan does not want to steal this gold but being
deprived of Freia the gods turn old and gray so Wotan,
with Loge, descends to the realm of the Nibelungs.

Scene III

Alberich, by power of the ring, has made himself
ruler of all his kind and has amassed a hoard of
treasure. He also forced Mime, his brother, to make
him a Tarnhelm, or wishing cap, which would make
the wearer invisible. Loge cunningly persuades him
to show off the powers of this cap and accordingly he
changes himself into a dragon and then a toad.
Immediately the gods seize him and take his treasures.

Scene IV

Alberich so resents having to yield the ring and
the Tarnhelm that he lays a curse on the ring. It shall
cause the death of everyone who owns it. Erda, goddess of wisdom, warns Wotan to yield the ring. As
soon as the giants get it they quarrel and Fasolt is
slain. Struck by the power of the curse, Wotan turns
all his thoughts to saving himself from his menacing
fate. Donner clears the air with a thunderstorm and
bids Froh to build a rainbow bridge to Valhalla. As
the gods are about to cross the bridge the voices of the

Rhinemaidens are heard below bewailing the loss of their gold.

See Poems.

For Leading Motives see the appendix, p. 187.

THE VALKYRIES
(*Die Walküre*)

First of the music-dramas composing the trilogy of *The Ring of the Nibelungs*, preceded by the prologue *Das Rheingold.*

CHARACTERS

Siegmund - - - - - - -	Tenor
Hunding - - - - - - -	Bass
Wotan - - - - - - - -	Baritone-bass
Sieglinde - - - - - - -	Soprano
Brünnhilde - - - - - -	Soprano
Fricka - - - - - - - -	Mezzo-soprano
Valkyrs - - - - - -	
Gerhilde	
Grimgerde	- Sopranos of
Helmwige	dramatic quality
Ortlinde	
Rossweise - - - - - -	Mezzo-soprano
Schwertleite - - - - -	Contralto
Siegrune - - - - - -	Contralto
Waltraute - - - - - -	Mezzo-soprano

TIME—Legendary

PLACE—Interior of Hunding's hut; a rocky height; the peak of a rocky mountain (the Brünnhilde rock)

Poem written in 1852, finished November of that year. Composition of music begun June 28, 1854. Act 1 completed Sept. 1, 1854; Act 2 begun Sept. 4,

113

completed Nov. 18, 1854; Act 3 begun Nov. 20, completed Dec. 27, 1854. Scoring started June, 1854. Act 1 finished Apr. 3, 1855; Act 2 finished Oct. 1 or 2, 1855; Act 3 finished Mar. 26, 1856. Full score published in 1873.

A large portion of the instrumentation was completed at 22 Portland Terrace, Regents Park, London. First engraved vocal score (Klindworth's original arrangement) 1865, by Schott & Co.

First produced at the Royal Court Theatre, Munich, on June 26, 1870.

ORIGINAL CAST

Siegmund - - - - -	Vogl
Hunding - - - - -	Bausewein
Wotan - - - - - -	Kindermann
Sieglinde - - - - -	Frau Vogl
Brünnhilde - - - -	Fräulein Stehle
Fricka - - - - - -	Fräulein Kaufmann

First authorized performance in the Festspielhaus at Bayreuth, Aug. 14, 1876.

ORIGINAL BAYREUTH CAST

Siegmund - - - - -	Albert Niemann
Hunding - - - - -	Joseph Niering
Wotan - - - - - -	Franz Betz
Sieglinde - - - - -	Josephin Scheffsky
Fricka - - - - - -	Friedericke Grün
Brünnhilde - - - -	Amalia Friedrich-Materna
Gerhilde - - - - -	Marie Haupt
Ortlinde - - - - -	Marie Lehmann
Waltraute - - - - -	Luise Jäide
Schwertleite - - - -	Johanna Jachmann-Wagner
Helmwige - - - - -	Lilli Lehmann

Siegrune - - - - - Antoinie Amann
Grimgerde - - - - - Hedwig Reicher-
                     Kindermann
Rossweise - - - - - Minna Lammert

First performance in America at the Academy of Music, New York, April 2, 1877.

CAST

Siegmund - - - - - Mr. Bischoff
Hunding - - - - - Mr. Blum
Wotan - - - - - - Mr. Preusser
Sieglinde - - - - - Mlle. Canissa
Fricka - - - - - - Mille. Listner
Brünnhilde - - - - Mme. Pappenheim

CONDUCTOR, Adolf Neuendorff

THE MUSIC-DRAMA
Argument

Act I

Siegmund, the son of Wotan in the form of a hero Wälse, fleeing from an enemy tribe, takes refuge in the hut of Hunding, another of his enemies and husband of Sieglinde.

Sieglinde gives Siegmund food and invites him to remain for the night. Hunding is bound by the laws of hospitality not to harm the guest until the morrow when he plans to kill him. He retires to his room for the night and partakes of his night brew into which Sieglinde has put a drug so that he may not awaken during the night. Siegmund and Sieglinde fall in love with each other and then discover that they are twin brother and sister. Sieglinde shows Siegmund a sword in the ash tree, the symbol of life, telling him that he may have it to protect himself if he is strong enough to draw it out. Siegmund discovers it is the magic sword

115

Wotan has plunged there and promised he would find when most he needed it. They elope during the night.

Act II

Fricka, goddess of marriage and wife of Wotan, appeals to him for justice to be done upon the infamous pair. Fricka remonstrates with Wotan and forces him to withhold protection from Siegmund and void the magic power of the sword. Brünnhilde, a valkyr and daughter of Wotan, had been sent by him to ride to Siegmund and inform him of his fate, but Brünnhilde is so won by the hero's noble courage that she disobeys Wotan's command and attempts to help Siegmund in his fight with Hunding. Wotan intervenes in the fight himself and causes the death of his beloved Siegmund and then slays Hunding. In his rage, he turns against Brünnhilde who then flees with Sieglinde. Brünnhilde flees to a band of Valkyries gathered on a mountain top for assistance, but is unsuccessful in her purpose.

Act III

She is pursued by the furious Wotan because of her disobedience. She does not fear his wrath so much for herself as she does for Sieglinde. In order to save Sieglinde she sends her away on the Valkyrie's fastest steed and promises her that she shall become the mother of Siegfried, the greatest hero of the world, and that he shall restore the sword of which she gives her the pieces. Brünnhilde remains to bear the brunt of Wotan's anger. He arrives and in his fury deprives Brünnhilde of her immortality and dooms her to lie in a charmed sleep until a man may wake and possess her. However, he concedes to her pleadings to place a protecting wall of fire around her so that only a hero may pass through. Both know secretly that this hero is to be the unborn Siegfried.

For Leading Motives see the appendix, p. 187.

SIEGFRIED

Originally called *Young Siegfried*. Second of the music-dramas composing *The Ring of the Nibelungs*.

CHARACTERS

Siegfried - - - - - - - Tenor
Mime - - - - - - - Tenor
Wotan (disguised as the
    Wanderer) - - - - - - Baritone-bass
Alberich - - - - - - - Baritone-bass
Fafner - - - - - - - - Bass
Erda - - - - - - - - - Contralto
Forest Bird - - - - - - Soprano
Brünnhilde - - - - - - Soprano

TIME—Legendary

PLACE—A rocky cave in the forest; deep
in the forest; wild region at foot
of a rocky mount; the Brünnhilde
rock.

Music begun at Zürich Sept. 22, 1856. Act I finished Apr. 1857. Act II, composition draft begun May 22, 1857, finished July 30. Most of Act II, up to the "Waldweben," written in that year, and the entire act completed at Munich June 21, 1865. Instrumentation completed at Triebschen, Feb. 23, 1869. Sketch of Act III finished in 1869. Score completed Feb. 5, 1871 and full score published in 1876. First engraved vocal score (Klindworth's original arrangement) published in 1871 by Schott & Co.

Performed first at the Festspielhaus, Bayreuth, on Aug. 16, 1876, under Hans Richter.

ORIGINAL CAST

The Wanderer - - - - Franz Betz
Siegfried - - - - Georg Unger

117

RING

Alberich - - - - - -	Carl Hill
Mime - - - - - - -	Carl Schlosser
Fafner - - - - - -	Franz von Reichen-berg
Brünnhilde - - - - -	Amalia Friedrich-Materna
Erda - - - - - - -	Luise Jäide
Forest Bird - - - - -	Lilli Lehmann

First performed in America at the Metropolitan Opera House, New York, Nov. 9, 1887.

Cast

The Wanderer - - - -	Emil Fischer
Siegfried - - - - -	Max Alvary
Alberich - - - - - -	Rudolph von Milde
Mime - - - - - - -	Herr Ferency
Fafner - - - - - -	Johannes Elmblad
Brünnhilde - - - - -	Lilli Lehmann
Erda - - - - - - -	Marianne Brandt
Forest Bird - - - - -	Auguste Seidl-Kraus

CONDUCTOR, Anton Seidl

THE MUSIC-DRAMA
Argument

Act I

Sieglinde, whom Brünnhilde had sent into the woods to escape the vengeance of Wotan, went to Nibelheim, the home of the Nibelungs, and was cared for by them. She died in giving birth to Siegfried. Mime, a Nibelung and brother of Alberich, brought up Siegfried because he believed that through the boy he could make himself the possessor of the Ring, knowing Siegfried was destined to kill Fafner and gain the Ring. Mime is known for the fine swords he makes but Siegfried

118

breaks them as if they were toys. One sword, however, Mime knows the boy could not break but neither is Mime able to weld together the fragments of that sword, Nothung. Mime tells Siegfried about his parents and the sword which his father left and of which his mother gave the two fragments to Mime as recompense for bringing up Siegfried. Siegfried demands that Mime forge it for him at once but the Wanderer, Wotan, has already visited Mime and told him that only one who has never known fear will be able to forge the sword. Mime tells this to Siegfried, who becomes impatient, grabs his father's sword and forges it successfully, much to Mime's awe.

Act II

Alberich watches the cave in the forest where Fafner guards the ring. Wotan appears and harasses Alberich by telling him that a hero is coming to rescue the Hoard; Fafner will die and the gold shall be his who shall seize it. Meanwhile, Mime, under the pretense of teaching Siegfried to fear, induces the boy to accompany him to the depths of the forest where a dragon, who is Fafner, guards the Nibelung treasures, including the ring. Here in the forest Siegfried becomes interested in the birds and makes them his friends. When Fafner comes out of his cave for water, Siegfried battles with him and slays him with his sword Nothung. Accidentally he tastes of the dragon's blood and by so doing is enabled to understand the speech of the birds. They tell him of Mime's plan to poison him and so obtain the treasure. Acting on this information Siegfried kills the traitor. A bird then tells him of a glorious bride who awaits him. She sleeps on a rocky height surrounded by fire. The bird flies before him and leads him to her.

Act III

Wotan, conscious of impending doom, seeks counsel of Erda but is unsuccessful in gaining the desired information. In his wanderings he meets Siegfried who asks of him the way to the rocky heights. Wotan refuses to give the information and puts his spear in the way so that Siegfried cannot pass. This arouses Siegfried's wrath and with Nothung he shatters the spear to pieces thereby taking all power away from Wotan. Siegfried, seeing the reflected fire in the clouds, reaches it, plunges through it, finds Brünnhilde, awakens her, woos and wins her.

See Poems; Siegfried's Death (Siegfried's Tod).

For Leading Motives see the appendix, p. 187.

TWILIGHT OF THE GODS
(Götterdämmerung)

Third of the music-dramas comprising *The Ring of the Nibelungs.*

CHARACTERS

Siegfried	Tenor
Gunther	Baritone
Alberich	Baritone
Hagen	Bass
Brünnhilde	Soprano
Gutrune	Soprano
Waltraute	Mezzo-soprano
Three Norns (Nornir)	Contralto, Mezzo-soprano and Soprano
Woglinde, Wellgunde, Flosshilde	Sopranos and Mezzo-soprano

TIME—Legendary

120

PLACE—Act 1: On the Brünnhilde rock;
Act 2: Gunther's castle on the
Rhine; Act 3: A wooded district
by the Rhine.

Poem written in 1848 as *Siegfried's Tod*; printed
in Vol. VI of *Gesammelte Schriften* (Vol. 8 of Ellis).
The first sketches of *Siegfried's Tod* are dated June,
1848. Music begun at Lucerne in 1870 and completed
at Bayreuth Nov. 1874. Sketch of Introduction and
Act I completed Jan. 20, 1871. Sketch of full score
finished at Bayreuth June 22, 1872. Instrumentation
completed Nov. 21, 1874. Full score published first in
1876. First engraved vocal score (Klindworth's
original arrangement) 1875, by Schott & Co.

First performed at Bayreuth, at the Festspielhaus,
on Aug. 17, 1876 under Hans Richter.

ORIGINAL CAST

Siegfried - - - -	Georg Unger
Gunther - - - -	Eugen Gura
Hagen - - - - -	Gustav Siehr
Alberich - - - -	Carl Hill
Brünnhilde - - - -	Amalia Friedrich-Materna
Gutrune - - - -	Mathilde Weckerlin
Waltraute - - - -	Luise Jäide
The Three Norns - -	Johanna Jachmann-Wagner
	Josephine Scheffsky
	Fredericke Grün
The Rhinemaidens -	Lilli Lehmann
	Marie Lehmann
	Minna Lammert

First performed in America at the Metropolitan
Opera House, New York, Jan. 25, 1888.

RING

CAST

Siegfried	- - - -	Albert Niemann
Gunther	- - - -	Adolf Robinson
Hagen	- - - - -	Emil Fischer
Alberich	- - - -	Rudolph von Milde
Brünnhilde	- - - -	Lilli Lehmann
Gutrune	- - - -	Auguste Seidl-Kraus
Woglinde	- - - -	Sophie Traubmann
Wellgunde	- - - -	Marianne Brandt
Flosshilde	- - - -	Louise Meisslinger

CONDUCTOR, Anton Seidl

THE MUSIC-DRAMA
Argument

Prelude

The scene takes place at night on Brünnhilde's rock. Three Norns entwine a golden rope of runes from one to another and fasten it to a fir tree and the rock. Soon it breaks and they descend to Erda because they know the end of the gods is at hand. At dawn Siegfried and Brünnhilde, with her horse, come from the cave. They proclaim their love for each other and to seal it Siegfried gives Brünnhilde the Ring in which lies the virtue of the deeds of valor he has wrought. In return, Brünnhilde gives him her horse and shield. Siegfried then leaves her to go to fresh exploits.

Act I

Siegfried comes to the Hall of the Gibichungs, on the Rhine, the dwelling of King Gunther, his sister Gutrune and their half-brother Hagen, son of Alberich. These three are desirous of power, therefore they give Siegfried a magic draught of forgetfulness. As a result, he swears blood brotherhood to Gunther, forgets Brünnhilde, falls in love with Gutrune and in return for her hand consents to go through the fire and bring Brünn-hilde as a wife for Gunther, who is unable to do so himself.

As Brünnhilde waits for Siegfried to return, her sister Waltraute visits her and implores her to restore the ring to the Rhinemaidens as the only means of saving the gods. Brünnhilde, being an outcast from Walhalla, regards her love-pledge to be more valuable than all the gods and refuses. Waltraute leaves in despair. Under power of the Tarnhelm Siegfried takes the likeness of Gunther and appears to Brünnhilde demand-ing that they be wed. She refuses; but after a violent struggle, during which he tears the Ring from her finger, he succeeds in wedding her but lays his sword Nothung between as his oath to Gunther demands.

Act II

Alberich, realizing that the gods will soon lose their power, visits his son Hagen and bids him strive to kill Siegfried and thereby obtain the ring. Siegfried, followed by Gunther and Brünnhilde, returns to the Gibichung's Hall. Hagen summons all the vassals to prepare for and rejoice at the double wedding. Brünn-hilde is brought face to face with Siegfried in his own self, sees the ring upon his finger and proclaims to all that she has been betrayed. Hagen purposely confuses the explanations and makes it appear that Siegfried has failed in his oath to Gunther. He finally persuades Brünnhilde, who is suffering great pangs of anguish because of her betrayal, and Gunther to consent to the murder of Siegfried. Gutrune is greatly grieved that he should die, so Hagen plans a method by which she will not know when he is killed.

Act III

While Siegfried is hunting near the Rhine, he is accosted by the Rhinemaidens who try to coax the ring from him. When they find that they are unsuccessful they tell him how it will cause his death but he does not take heed. Soon the rest of the hunting party, including Hagen and Gunther, join him. While they are carousing and Siegfried is telling the story of his life Hagen spears him in the back, kills him and after the body has been brought to the Hall, to the accompaniment of a wonderful funeral dirge, he claims the ring. Gunther also claims it and as a result is killed by Hagen.

Brünnhilde orders a funeral pyre to be built, by the river side, to consume the body of the great hero. She follows Siegfried's body and before it is burned takes the ring from his finger and puts it on hers, mounts his horse and rides onto the pyre, there to burn with her lover. The river rises and the Rhinemaidens at last regain their ring from the ashes, Hagen being drowned in an attempt to seize it. A ruddy glare is seen in the sky. The Dusk of the Gods has come and Walhalla burns with all its array of heroes and gods.

See Letters and Minor Essays, No. 7.

For Leading Motives see the appendix, p. 187.

Ritter, Frau Julie. Friend of Wagner in Zürich, supplying him with money regularly till the end of 1856. Mother of Karl Ritter, musician and friend of Richard Wagner. A resident of Dresden. She had left her home at Narva, early in the eighteen forties, in the Russian Baltic provinces to reside at Dresden for the education of her sons Karl and Alexander.

Ritter, Karl. Son of Frau Julie Ritter; a musician. First person to see MS. of *Young Siegfried*. Suggested a sketch for the dramatic treatment of *Tristan and Isolde* and thereby drew Wagner's attention to the material for that poem. Feeling insulted by Liszt when at Wagner's house on one occasion, he removed from Zürich and settled permanently at

Lausanne. This resulted in an estrangement between Wagner and Ritter which later was patched up. He accompanied Wagner to Italy. Parted with him at Venice, Ritter later going to Naples.

Rivalin. King of Parmenia. Marries Blanchefleur. See *Tristan and Isolde.*

Roche, Edmond. Born at Calais, Feb. 20, 1828. A customs officer. He died of consumption at Paris, Dec. 16, 1861 very soon after the performance of *Tannhäuser* at the Paris Grand Opera. Translator of *Tannhäuser;* friend and visitor of Wagner in Paris.

Rochlitz, Hofrath. Managing Director of the Gewandhaus Concerts at Leipzig. Editor of the *Allgemeine Musikalische Zeitung.*

Röckel, August. Friend and assistant to Wagner. Called by Wagner "the companion of my solitude." Assistant Conductor at the Dresden Opera in 1843-49. Born Dec. 1, 1814 at Graz. Son of Prof. Joseph August Röckel, tenor and impressario, who successfully introduced German opera into Paris and London. August died at Buda-Pesth on June 18, 1876.
A nephew of Hummel, famous composer and pianist. He was tutored by Beethoven for the part of Florestan in *Fidelio.* Composed the opera *Farinelli.* He was the first person, with Uhlig, to see the pages of *Lohengrin.* Imprisoned for participation in the Dresden revolution of May 1849, he was pardoned through the efforts of Wagner, after serving thirteen years, 1849-62. Editor of the Dresden *Volksblatt.*

Rössig, Anna Sophia. Daughter of Master Christoph Rössig, flour-mill operator at Dahlen. Wife of Samuel Wagner, the younger.

Rossini, A Remembrance of. See Notices, No. 3.

Rossini's "Stabat Mater." See German Musician in Paris, A. No. 7.

Rossweise. A character in *The Ring*; mezzo-soprano. A valkyrie. *Die Walküre*, Act 3. Rôle created at first Festspielhaus performance by Minna Lammert.

Rückblick auf die Bühnenfestspiele das Jahres 1876, Ein. See Retrospect of the Stage-Festivals of 1876, A.

"Rule Britannia" Overture. Listed in Musical Works. Written at Königsberg, 1836 or 1837. Performed there March 1837. Published in 1904. A set of parts, with the score, is at Bayreuth.

S

Sachs, Hans. One of the mastersingers in *Die Meistersinger*; bass. A cobbler. Acts 1, 2, 3. Rôle created by Betz.

"Hans Sachs I took as a representation of the art-productive spirit of the Folk, and set him in contrast to the petty-fogging bombast of the other Mastersingers; to whose ridiculous pedantry of *tabulatur* and prosody I gave concrete expression in the figure of the 'marker'."

Richard Wagner, in the original sketch dated Marienbad, July 16, 1845.

He was a historical character, a mastersinger, born at Nuremberg in 1494, died in 1576. His first wife died Mar. 18, 1560. He married again on Sept. 2, 1561.

St. Nicholas School. Leipzig. Wagner was entered at this school Jan. 21, 1828.

St. Thomas School. Leipzig. Wagner was entered at this school in June, 1830.

Saracen Woman, The. P.W. 8. (1841-43) Opera
in five acts.

CHARACTERS

Fatima	Soprano
Manfred	Tenor
Lancia	Bass
Nurredin	Tenor
Burello	Bass
Ali	Bass
Feretrio	Bass

Scene laid in Capua.

Sketched by Wagner in Paris in 1841; scenic draft
completed as an operatic text for Frau Schröder-
Devrient, later mislaid. A copy of the manuscript
was found among the papers of Domkapell-Meister
Greith, of Munich, 1888. It was given to Herr
Heinrich Porges who transferred it to the Wahnfried
archives. Printed in *Bayreuther Blätter* January,
1889.

Sarazenin, Die. See Saracen Woman, The.

Savitri. See Prakriti.

Saxe, Marie (Marie Constance Sasse). (1838-1907)
Belgian soprano. Pupil of Mme. Ugalde. Sang the
role of Elizabeth in *Tannhäuser* in Paris, March 13,
1861. In 1859 sang at the Paris Lyrique, 1860 at
the Opera, from 1871 in Italian cities, and after 1882
at Brussels.

Sayn-Wittgenstein, Princess Carolyne. Born, 1819,
Carolyne Iwanowska, daughter of a wealthy Polish
landowner. Married Prince Nicolaus von Sayn-
Wittgenstein in 1836. Liszt met her while on tour in
February, 1847 at Kieff, Russia. Prince Nicolaus,
a protestant, obtained a divorce from her and married
again. Carolyne, being a member of the Roman

Church, was forbidden by the Pope to marry Liszt. In April, 1848, she left Russia and established herself in Liszt's home in June in Weimar. Died 1887; buried in Rome.

Schausspieler und Sänger, Über. See Actors and Singers.

Schindelmeisser, Louis. (1811-1864) Friend of Wagner. Kapellmeister at the Königstadt Theatre in Berlin. Step-brother of Heinrich Dorn.

Schlesinger. A publishing house in Berlin founded by Adolf Martin Schlesinger, 1795. Founded the *Berliner Allgemeine Musikalisches Zeitung.* His eldest son, Moritz Adolf, founded a music business in Paris in 1834, becoming a leader among French publishers. He induced Habeneck, conductor of the Paris Conservatory orchestra, to try the *Eine Faust Ouverture.* Accepted several articles from Wagner for the *Gazette Musicale.*

Schmerzen. See Five Poems.

Schnorr von Carolsfeld, Ludwig. Tenor. Created part of Tristan at Munich June 10, 1865, his wife as Isolde. Born July 2, 1836 at Munich. Son of Julius Schnorr von Carolsfeld, a painter. Was instructed in music by Julius Otto at Dresden. Studied for the stage under Eduard Devrient at Carlsruhe. Married Malwine Garrigues (born Dec. 7, 1825). Sang in opera and festivals at Mainz, Düsseldorf, Weisbaden and Frankfort. Wagner heard him at Carlsruhe in 1862 as Lohengrin. Died July 21, 1865; buried in Dresden. His wife died at Carlsruhe Feb. 8, 1904.

See My Recollections of Ludwig Schnorr of Carolsfeld.

Schröder-Devrient, Wilhelmine. Born at Hamburg, according to her own account, on Dec. 6, 1804. A talented but notoriously amorous opera singer—soprano—who made a great impression upon Wagner. He said, "Whenever I conceived a character, I saw her." Daughter of Friedrich Schröder, a baritone, and Antoinette Sophie Schröder (Burger), a celebrated tragédienne, known as the German Siddons. Married Karl Devrient, an actor, in 1823, by whom she had four children. The marriage was dissolved in 1828. Became infatuated with a Saxon officer, Lieut. von Döring, in 1842. The infatuation lasted seven years. Was married to him Aug. 29, 1847. The marriage was dissolved and in 1850 she married Herr von Bock, a cultured gentleman.

First Senta in *The Flying Dutchman* and created the rôle of Venus in *Tannhäuser*. Appeared as Adriano Colonna in *Rienzi*. Appeared on the stage for the last time May 16, 1847. Died at Coburg, Jan. 21, 1860. There is a life of her by Alfred von Wolzogen. A tribute to her is given by Wagner in his *Actors and Singers*.

Schwanhilde. A character in *Wieland the Smith*.

Schwartz, Hans. One of the mastersingers in *Die Meistersinger*; bass. A stocking-weaver. Acts 1, 3. Rôle created by Graffer.

Schweizerhof, Hotel. At Lucerne, on the Schweizerhof Quay. In this hotel the entire third act of *Tristan* was written. The proprietor was Herr Seegesser.

Schwertleite. A character in *The Ring*; contralto. A valkyrie.
Die Walküre, Act 3. Rôle created at first Fest-

129

spielhaus performance by Johanna Jachmann-Wagner.

Scribe, (Augustin) Eugène. French dramatist and the best librettist of his time. Born in Paris, Dec. 25, 1791. Librettist of Meyerbeer's *Les Huguenots* and many other operas. A draft of an opera was sent to him by Wagner but never performed. Also copy of the score of *Das Liebesverbot.* Died in Paris Feb. 21, 1861.

Seelisberg. Residence of Wagner, Kurhaus Sonnenberg, Canton Uri, on the shore of Lake Lucerne opposite to Brunnen, July 11 to Aug. 15, 1855.

Semper's Theatre. Dresden. Here *Rienzi, The Flying Dutchman* and *Tannhäuser* were first produced. Opened in April 1841. Burnt down in 1869. See full description by the designer, with plans, in *Das Königliche Hoftheatre zu Dresden,* by Gottfried Semper; Braunschweig, 1849.

Senta. A character in *The Flying Dutchman*; soprano. Daughter of Daland. Act 2, scenes 1, 2, 3; Act 3, scene 2. Rôle created by Schröder-Devrient.

Shall We Hope? P.W. 6. Published in the *Bayreuther Blätter* May, 1879.

Shepherd. A character in *Tannhäuser*; soprano. Act 1, scene 3. Rôle created by Fräulein Thiele.

Shepherd. A character in *Tristan and Isolde.* Act 3, scenes 1, 3.

Sieger, Die. A Buddhistic drama sketched by Wagner in 1856, but abandoned. See Victors, The.

Siegfried. A character in *The Ring*; tenor. Son of Siegmund and Sieglinde.
Siegfried, Acts 1, 2, 3. Rôle created by Georg Unger.

Götterdämmerung, Prelude, Acts 1, 2, 3. Rôle created by Georg Unger.

Siegfried Idyll. Composed by Wagner in 1871[1] at Triebschen, in honor of his son and to celebrate his wife's birthday. The leading themes are taken from *Siegfried,* combined with an old German cradle-song, *Schlafe Kindchen.* Score published in 1878 by Schott. The purpose, according to Wagner, was to express the pure and serene sentiments which filled one's mind, when gazing upon a sleeping infant. Dedicated to his wife Cosima. Sometimes called *Morceau de l'Escalier* in remembrance of its first execution. Played in 1871 at Mannheim and in 1877 at the Court of the Grand Duke Meiningen under the composer's direction. Listed in Musical Works.

Siegfried's Death. Text of a drama by Wagner which was afterward developed into *The Ring of the Nibelungs.* Poem written Nov. 1848.

CHARACTERS

Siegfried, Gunther, Hagen, Alberich, Brünn-hilde, Gutrune, Three Norns, Three Water-Nixies, Valkyries.

SCENE: By the Rhine.

Drama written at Zürich about June 29, 1851. Changed to three dramas with a prologue, completed in 1852-53. *Siegfried's Tod* was never set to music. It was, some twenty-five years later, merged into *Götterdämmerung.* A manuscript draft of about 20 pages, dated Oct. 20, 1848, is preserved at Wahnfried. Original of poem is printed in Vol. II of *Gesammelte Schriften* (Vol. 8 of Ellis).

See Ring of the Nibelungs, The.

[1] Lawrence Gilman gives the date as November, 1870.

Siegfried's Funeral March. Act 3 of *Götterdämmerung*.

Siegfried's Rhine Journey. Played by the orchestra between the Prelude and opening of Act I of *Götterdämmerung*.

Siegfried's Tod (Death). See Siegfried's Death.

Sieglinde. A character in *The Ring*; soprano. Wife of Siegmund. Twin-sister to Siegmund, daughter of Wotan in the form of a hero, Wälse.
> *Die Walküre*, Acts 1, 2. Rôle created by Frau Vogl.

Siegmund. A character in *The Ring*; tenor. A warrior; twin-brother to Sieglinde; son of Wotan in the form of a hero, Wälse.
> *Die Walküre*, Acts, 1, 2. Rôle created by Vogl.

Siegrune. A character in *The Ring*; contralto. A valkyrie.
> *Die Walküre*, Act 3. Rôle created at first Festspielhaus performance by Antoinie Amann.

Slaughter of the Innocents, The. Play by Ludwig Geyer, step-father of Richard Wagner. It was well known in Germany. On Wagner's sixtieth birthday his family at Bayreuth surprised him with a performance of this play.

Sleep, My Child (Dors, mon enfant). Listed in Musical Works.

Sonata, B ♭. Listed in Musical Works. Opus 1. Written 1831. Published 1832 by Breitkopf & Härtel.

Songs. See Musical Works.

Sorrows. See Five Poems, No. 4.

Special Cantata. Listed in Musical Works. Written for unveiling of bronze statue representing King Friedrich Augustus at Dresden June 7, 1843. Unpublished.

Speech at Weber's Last Resting Place. P.W. 7.

Spinning Chorus. Act 2, scene 1, of *The Flying Dutchman*.

Spohr's "Jessonda" at Leipzig. P.W. 6. Published in *Musikalisches Wochenblatt* Jan. 1875.

Spontini, Mementoes of. P.W. 3.

Spring Song. Siegmund's air in *Die Walküre*, Act 1. The Liebeslied.

Staat und Religion, Über. See State and Religion, On.

Stand Still. See Five Poems, No. 2.

State and Religion, On. P.W. 4. Written at the request of King Ludwig II of Bavaria in 1864. Printed in 1873, in Vol. VIII of *Gesammelte Schriften* (Collected Works). He wrote this at his villa on Lake Starnberg, near Munich. In this article, art is held to be the panacea for all ills. He treats in this of the functions of kings, patriotism, illusions, the press, faith, dogma, and other topics.

Steersman. A character in *Tristan and Isolde*. Act 3, scene 3.

Stehe still. See Stand Still.

Stein, H. von. Private tutor of Siegfried Wagner; later, teacher at the University of Halle and Berlin. Collaborator with C. F. Glasenapp in preparation of the *Wagner Lexikon*. Died June 20, 1887.

Stipendiary Fund, The. P.W. 6. Open letter to Herr Friedrich Schön of Worms. Published in the

Bayreuther Blätter July 1882. Suggested by Richard Wagner as a fund for enabling the needy to attend the Bayreuth performances. It was started by Herr Schön and by 1883 had amounted to £156. A Stipend-foundation was at that time established and on Oct. 1, 1876 its capital had reached 28,000 marks.

Stolzing, Walther von. See Walther von Stolzing.

Sulzer, Jacob. A local office holder in Zürich, friend of Wagner.

Sundry Sketches and Fragments. P.W. 8.

Symphony in C major. Composed in 1832 and performed at the Leipzig Gewandhaus on Jan. 10, 1833. Performed at Prague in the summer of 1832. Also in December of that year at the Euterpe. Score lost by Mendelssohn who, when asked by Wagner to conduct it, put it aside. In 1872 the orchestral parts were found in an old trunk left by Wagner in Dresden. Performed on Dec. 24, 1882, at Venice. Produced by Anton Seidl in Chickering Hall, New York, Mar. 2, 1888.

See Youthful Symphony, A. Listed in Musical Works.

T

Tannenbaum, Der. See Fir Tree, The.

Tannhäuser. A character in *Tannhäuser*; tenor. A bard of Thuringia. Act 1, scenes 2, 3, 4; Act 2, scenes 2, 4; Act 3, scene 3. Rôle created by Tichatschek. See Ofterdingen, Heinrich von.

Tannhäuser. Dramatic opera in three acts. Full title, *Tannhäuser und der Sängerkrieg auf Wartburg* (Tannhäuser and the Contest of Song on the Wartburg). Original title, intended, "Der Venusberg" (The Hill of Venus).

CHARACTERS

Hermann, Landgrave of Thuringia -	Bass

Knights and Minnesinger

Tannhäuser - - - - - - - -	Tenor
Wolfram von Eschenbach - - - -	Baritone
Walter von der Vogelweide - - -	Tenor
Biterolf - - - - - - - - - -	Bass
Heinrich der Schreiber - - - - -	Tenor
Reinmar von Zweter - - - - -	Bass
Elizabeth, niece of the Landgrave -	Soprano
Venus - - - - - - - - - - -	Soprano
A Young Shepherd - - - - - -	Soprano
Four Noble Pages - - - - - -	Soprano and Alto

TIME—Early 13th Century

PLACE—Near Eisenach, in Thuringia, and the castle of Wartburg.

Outline of book completed at Teplitz in 1842. Scenario worked out in the Bohemian mountains in 1842, in a note book, now in the Burrell collection, bearing date June 22 and July. Poem finished May 22, 1843. Music begun at Dresden in summer of 1843. First act written between July 1843 and January 1844; second act in the summer and fall of 1844; third act prior to the end of 1844. Opera completed in April 1844. Instrumentation finished by April 1845. Pianoforte arrangement by Josef Rubenstein. Revisions for the Paris production composed in 1860-61. Score published by Meser of Dresden.

SOURCES

Inspired by Hoffmann's *Sängerkrieg*, legends of Parzival, Lohengrin and Tannhäuser. Also the *German Folkbook of Tannhäuser*, as mentioned in *A Communication to My Friends*. The character of

Tannhäuser in the opera was taken mainly from a bard, Henry von Ofterdingen, a native of Thuringia. He figured in the famous battle of the Bards at Wartburg.

First performance in Dresden at the Royal Saxon Court Theatre on Oct. 19, 1845 under Wagner.

ORIGINAL CAST

Hermann, Landgrave of Thuringia	Dettmer
Tannhäuser	Tichatschek
Wolfram von Eschenbach	Mitterwurzer
Walther von der Vogelweide	Schloss
Biterolf	Wächter
Heinrich der Schreiber	Gurth
Reinmar von Zweter	Risse
Elizabeth, niece of the Landgrave	Fräulein Johanna Wagner
Venus	Mme. Schröder-Devrient
A Young Shepherd	Fräulein Thiele

First performance in America at the Stadt-Theatre, New York, April 4, 1859.

CAST

Hermann	Graff
Tannhäuser	Pickaneser
Wolfram	Lehmann
Walther	Lotti
Biterolf	Urchs
Heinrich der Schreiber	Bolten
Reinmar von Zweter	Brandt
Elizabeth	Mme. Siedenburg

Venus - - - - - - - Mme. Pickaneser
Shepherd - - - - - -   (not given)
CONDUCTOR, Carl Bergmann

Produced in Zürich Feb. 1855, Wagner conducting. At the Imperial Opera, Vienna, in 1859. In Paris, by order of the Emperor Napoleon III March 13, 1861, Albert Niemann in the title role, Morelli as Wolfram, Mme. Tedesco as Venus, Marie Saxe as Elizabeth. Owing to the tremendous noise made by hunting whistles in the hands of members of the Jockey Club the performance was a failure.

The overture was the first piece of Wagner's music played publicly in England.

THE OPERA

Argument

Act I

The curtain rises on the interior of the Venus- berg—Mount of Venus—showing a wide grotto, a waterfall plunging between rocks, a lake in which Naiads are bathing and sirens recline on the banks. Venus reclines in front of the grotto and Tannhäuser kneels before her, charmed, while Satyrs, Fawns, Nymphs and pursuing youths fill the stage with move- ment. Presently Tannhäuser appears to awaken from a dream and memories recur of the earth he has left. Venus again exercises her power of charm and he takes his harp and sings a hymn in her praise. He soon weakens and implores her to permit his departure. Her anger becomes aroused and she bids him begone, saying that neither heaven nor earth can save him and when both have rejected him he will return to her. The scene changes to Wartburg and Tannhäuser finds himself in the presence of a young shepherd who sings the popular legend of the goddess Holda. Pilgrims enter, on their

137

way to Rome, to obtain absolution for their sins. Their chant inspires Tannhäuser with a sense of his own sinfulness and he falls on his knees. The Landgrave of Thuringia, with his followers, appears and they recognize the praying man as the bard Henry, who disappeared the previous year. Tannhäuser wishes to leave them but they entreat him to remain because Wolfram, a brother bard and Tannhäuser's dearest friend, tells him that Elizabeth, the niece of the Landgrave, reciprocates his passion.

Act II

Elizabeth enters the Hall of the Muses in the Castle of Wartburg overjoyed at the return of Tannhäuser, who appears with Wolfram in the background. He throws himself at Elizabeth's feet and a love scene ensues, at the end of which the Landgrave appears. The Contest of the Bards follows, using the chosen theme "What is Love?" The victor of this contest is to receive the hand of Elizabeth. Wolfram begins and his song treats the subject from that higher point of view which is the distinguishing trait of the German love-poems of the middle ages. Tannhäuser depicts love as a mere sensuous passion. His verses are at first received with cold silence but when he vows he has visited the Mount of Venus, the indignation of the assembly becomes so great that they are about to kill him. Elizabeth intervenes, begs his life and implores him to repent. The Landgrave bids him start to Rome with the Pilgrims. Tannhäuser is overcome with grief and remorse and joins the Pilgrims.

Act III

The Valley of Wartburg. It is autumn and evening is descending. Elizabeth is seen prostrate, praying before the shrine of the Virgin. Wolfram approaches her from the wooded heights and in the distance are heard the Pilgrims, returning from Rome, having obtained absolution. Elizabeth eagerly looks among them for Tannhäuser but being disappointed returns to prayer and then enters the castle. Wolfram seats himself and plays on his harp, apostrophizing the evening star. Tannhäuser enters, worn and excited. Wolfram recognizes him and is horrified to learn that he has not obttained absolution but is still more terrified at hearing of his intention to return to Venus. Tannhäuser invokes the goddess and she triumphantly appears. Wolfram tries to restrain him from joining her but all efforts are useless until Tannhäuser, seeing that Elizabeth is dying and prays for him, finally repents. At this point Venus disappears, the Pilgrims and Bards descend the mountain carrying the dead body of Elizabeth. Tannhäuser, overcome with grief, flings himself on the corpse and expires.

See Explanatory Programmes; Music of the Future; Performing of Tannhäuser, On the; Report on the Production of Tannhäuser in Paris, A. For Leading Motives see the appendix, p. 187.

For an interpretation see Liszt, *Complete Works,* III, 2, *Richard Wagner;* Breitkopf & Härtel.

Tarnhelm. A wishing cap. In *The Ring;* made by Mime at the behest of his brother Alberich.

Tausig, Carl. Pianist, friend of Wagner. He made the piano arrangement of *Die Meistersinger,* as well as composed numerous other works. Said to have been, after Liszt, the best pianist of his time. Born at Warsaw, Nov. 4, 1841. Taught first by his father Aloys Tausig, a professional pianist. Died of typhoid fever, at Leipzig, July 17, 1871.

Tedesco, Fortunata. Soprano. Sang the role of Venus in *Tannhäuser* at Paris, March 13, 1861. Born Dec. 14, 1826 at Mantua. Made her debut in 1844 at Milan. Sang at Vienna, Paris, Lisbon, Madrid and in America. She retired in 1866.

Telramund. See Frederick of Telramund.

Teplitz. Wagner resided here June 1842; lodgings on a farm, "Zur Eiche," near the Turna Garden.

Thammenhain. Birthplace of Samuel Wagner, near Wurzen. The name has been interpreted as "Damian's grove." In 1284 it is found in the form "Tannen-hain," or "Fir-grove." The parish lies on the Thorgau road, in a hilly and wooded country.

Theatre at Zürich, A. P.W. 3. Published in Zürich, 1851.

Theatre Reform. P.W. 8. Published in *Dresdener Anzeiger* Jan. 16, 1849.

Thetis. The name of a small merchant vessel of 106 tons, on which Wagner and his wife sailed for London from Pillau, in Prussia. The vessel was Prussian-owned. Captain Wulff. Sailed probably July 18, arriving at London Aug. 12, 1839.

Tichatschek, Joseph Aloys. Celebrated tenor. Created part of Rienzi on Oct. 20, 1842, and Tannhäuser on Oct. 19, 1845. Born July 11, 1807 at Ober Weckelsdorf, in Bohemia. Began to study medicine but changed to music, receiving instruction from Ciccimara, a well-known Italian teacher. Became acquainted in 1837 with Schröder-Devrient with whom he had a long and intimate friendship. He retired in 1870. Died at Blasewitz near Dresden, Jan. 18, 1886.

Tintagel. Seat of King Marke's court in *Tristan and Isolde*.

Titurel. A character in *Parsifal*; bass. Former ruler of the kingdom of the Grail. Acts 1, 3. Rôle created by Kindermann.

To the German Army before Paris. A Poem. P.W. 5. Written in Jan. 1871.

To the Kingly Friend. Poem. P.W. 4. Written in the summer of 1864.

Toast at the Tercentenary of the Royal Kapell at Dresden. P.W. 7. Written in 1848.

Träume. See Five Poems, No. 5.

Triebschen. A promontory on a point of land on the banks of the lake near Lucerne where Wagner lived for six years, moving thence to Bayreuth. He had left Munich in December 1865 and a few weeks later found a house in an isolated section—Hof Triebschen.

Trinkspruch. See Toast at the Tercentenary of the Royal Kapell, etc.

Tristan.. A character in *Tristan and Isolde*; tenor. A Cornish knight, nephew to King Marke. Act 1, scenes 2, 6, 7; Act 2, scenes 2, 3; Act 3, scenes 1, 2, 3, 4. Rôle created by Ludwig Schnorr von Carolsfeld.

Tristan and Isolde. Music-drama in three acts.

CHARACTERS

Tristan, a Cornish knight, nephew to King Marke	Tenor
King Marke, of Cornwall	Bass
Isolde, an Irish princess	Soprano
Kurwenal, one of Tristan's retainers	Baritone
Melot, a courtier	Baritone
Brangäne, Isolde's attendant	Mezzo-soprano

Shepherd - - - - - - - - - Tenor
Sailor - - - - - - - - - - Tenor
Helmsman - - - - - - - - - Baritone

TIME—Legendary

PLACE—A ship at sea; outside King
Marke's palace, Cornwall; the
platform at Kanoël, Tristan's
castle in Brittany.

Poem written at Zürich 1857. Prose draft begun
Aug. 20 and completed Sept. 18. Prelude composi-
tion outlined Oct. 1, 1857. Pencilled composition-
draft dated: Act 1, Oct. 1 to Dec. 21, 1857; Act 2,
May 4 to July 1, 1858; Act 3, Lucerne, Apr. 9 to
July 16, 1859, written in the Hotel Schweizerhof.

Orchestral sketches: Act 1, Nov. 5, 1857 to Jan. 13,
1858; Act 2, July 5, 1858 at Zürich to March 9, 1859
at Venice; Act 3, May 1 to July 19, 1859, Lucerne.

Fair copy of score completed Saturday, Aug. 6,
1859. Pianoforte arrangement by Hans von Bülow.
Score sent to Breitkopf & Härtel Aug. 7, 1859.
Prelude first performed under von Bülow at Prague
Mar. 12, 1859.

First performance of the entire work at Munich
on June 10, 1865, conductor von Bülow.

ORIGINAL CAST

Tristan - - - - - Ludwig Schnorr von
Carolsfeld
Kurwenal - - - - Mitterwurzer
Melot - - - - - - Heinrich
Marke - - - - - Zottmayer
Isolde - - - - - - Mme. Schnorr von
Carolsfeld
Brangäne - - - - Mlle. Deinet

First performance in America at the Metropolitan Opera House, New York, on Dec. 1, 1886.

CAST

Tristan - - - - - Albert Niemann
Kurwenal - - - - Adolph Robinson
Melot - - - - - - Rudolph von Milde
Marke - - - - - Emil Fischer
Isolde - - - - - - Lilli Lehmann
Brangäne - - - - Marianne Brandt
Shepherd - - - - Otto Kemlitz
Sailor - - - - - - Max Alvary
Helmsman - - - - Emil Sänger

CONDUCTOR, Anton Seidl

Supposed inspirer was Mathilde Wesendonck, his friend living on the shores of the lake at Zürich where he lived from April, 1857 to August, 1858.

SOURCES

Old legend of the Arthurian cycle; poem "Tristan de Leonois," dating from 1190; a version of the old English cycle of legends written by Swinburne; Old French version of Thomas of Brittany. An Anglo-Norman direct source was the Teutonic form of the poem by Gottfried of Strassburg, a German, about 1210, High-German translation by Herman Kurz. The story came to his attention in 1854 while at work on *Die Walküre*.

Legendary

Rivalin, King of Parmenia, marries Blanchefleur, sister of King Marke in Cornwall. Rivalin is killed in battle and Blanchefleur's sorrow is so great that she dies, in the fortress of Kanoël, in giving birth to Tristan.

Tristan is brought up by his tutor Kurvenal. He visits King Marke's court at Tintagel, is recognized as

143

the King's nephew and treated with great honor. After he returns from a war in Parmenia he learns that Cornwall has been conquered by the Irish King Gurmun, whose brother-in-law, Morold, has come to collect tribute agreed upon. Tristan slays him in combat and sends his head to Ireland in scorn and defiance. Tristan received a poisoned wound from Morold's sword and has to go to Ireland to be treated by the magic art of Isot, wife of Gurmun. He visits Ireland in the guise of a merchant named Tantris, is healed and made tutor of the Queen's daughter, Isot the Fair. Later he returns to Cornwall and becomes involved in political complications. A party among the nobles is bent on deposing the childless old King Marke. Tristan, his nephew, is heir to the throne but for his own safety persuades King Marke to marry, proposing Isot the Fair (Isolde) as bride. He goes to Ireland again. He wins the country's gratitude by slaying a dragon that is ravaging the land but is recognized by the two Isots as Tantris. They find a notch in his sword which corresponds with a splinter left in Morold's head. Thus Tristan is revealed as Morold's slayer. Isot the Fair goes to slay Tristan but he buys his life with a promise to find her a rich husband.

The Queen gives Brangäne, Isot's maid, a love-philtre which is to be secretly given to King Marke and Isot on their wedding day. Isolde (Isot the Fair), Brangäne and Tristan set sail from Ireland together but Isolde does not conceal her hatred for Tristan. One day, on the ship, they accidentally drink the philtre and fall violently in love with each other. The lovers deceive the old King until finally Tristan has to leave court. He goes to Sussex, where he falls in love with and marries the Duke's daughter, Isot of the White Hand. Finally, Tristan is wounded in battle. Isot of Ireland is the only one who can heal him. She is sent for.

The messenger who has gone on the quest is instructed to hoist a blue and white sail if Isot returns with him, a black one if she does not. The blue and white sail is hoisted but the jealous Isot of the White Hand tells Tristan it is a black sail. He dies and Isot the Fair after him, holding him in her embrace. Isot of the White Hand buries them on opposite sides of the church so that even in death they should not be united; but an oak tree grows from each grave and the branches of the two meet over the roof of the church.

The Music-Drama
Argument

Act I

Tristan, a knight of Cornwall, is conveying Isolde, an Irish princess, to Cornwall as a bride for his uncle, King Marke. He has fallen in love with her but loyal to his mission conceals his passion. At his seeming inattention Isolde in anger attempts to poison herself and him but Brangäne changes the draught for a love-potion, which serves to increase their passion beyond control.

Act II

Isolde has wed King Marke but keeps trysts with Tristan. During one of these they are detected through the betrayal of Tristan by Melot, a jealous friend. King Marke reproaches him bitterly and Tristan, cut to the heart, engages Melot in battle and is mortally wounded.

Act III

Kurvenal, Tristan's retainer, has taken his wounded master to his native home in Brittany for tender care. Isolde, because of her skill in the healing art, has been sent for. In excitement at her coming Tristan's death is hastened and he expires in her arms. King Marke,

TRI-VAL

who has followed Isolde, learns how matters stand and
offers to reunite the lovers, but it is too late. Isolde
in transcendental emotion sings about the vision that
only she beholds and falls lifeless on the body of her
lover. In death alone they are united.

The pith of the Tristan "idea" as conceived by
Wagner is contained in programme notes for a Vienna
concert, Dec. 27, 1863, which he prepared, as follows:
(This date is given by Glasenapp but the correct date
seems to be Dec. 26, 1862).

TRISTAN UND ISOLDE

a) Prelude   (Love-death)
     (*Vorspiel*)   (*Liebestod*)

Tristan as bridal envoy conducts Isolde to his uncle
King. They love each other. From the most stifled
moan of quenchless longing, from the faintest tremour
to unpent avowal of a hopeless love, the heart goes
through each phase of unvictorious battling with its
inner fever, till, swooning back upon itself, it seems
extinguished as in death.

b) Conclusion   (Transfigurement)
     (*Schluss-satz*)   (*Verklärung*)

Yet, what fate divided for this life, in death revives
transfigured: the gate of union opens. Above the
corpse of Tristan, dying Isolde sees transcendent
consummation of their passionate desire (*des
glühenden Sehnens*), eternal union in unmeasured
realms, not bond nor barrier, indivisible!

Wagner called it "the simplest but fullest-blooded
musical conception."

See Invitation to the Production of *Tristan* in
    Munich; Music of the Future. For Leading
    Motives see the appendix, p. 187.

Two Grenadiers, The. Listed in Musical Works. (*Les deux Grenadiers*). (Heine's *Die beiden grenadiere*). Paris, 1839. Dedicated to Heine. Music fits the French version.

U

Uhlig, Theodor. Friend and assistant of Wagner, his first journalistic champion and the first Wagnerite. Born at Wurzen, near Leipzig, Feb. 15, 1822. King Friedrich August II in 1837 placed him at the music-school in Dessau. A composer who wrote almost a hundred vocal and instrumental pieces. He assisted Wagner materially in promoting the publication of his works. Most of the *Letters to Dresden Friends* were addressed to him and he was Wagner's chief epistolary correspondent. He wrote articles for the *Neue Zeitschrift für Musik* and made a pianoforte edition of *Lohengrin.* Died Jan. 3, 1853.

University of Leipzig. Wagner enrolled as *studiosus musicae* Feb. 23, 1831.

Upon the Completion of Siegfried. See Poems, No. 2.

V

Valhalla. Castle of refuge for the gods in *The Ring.* Built by the giants at the behest of Wotan.

Valkyries, The. Characters in *The Ring*; sopranos, mezzo-sopranos and contraltos. Wish-maidens or corpse-choosers. Nine daughters of Wotan, by Erda, the earth goddess. See also Ring of the Nibelungs, The.

Van der Decken. Name of the captain of an Amsterdam vessel mentioned in a version of a legend printed in *Blackwood's Magazine* in May 1821, which provided the original story of *The Flying Dutchman.*

Venice. Residence of Wagner, Palazzo Vendramini on the Grand Canal. It was built before the discovery of America (1481). Here he had a suite of 28 rooms on the first story. It belonged to the Estate of the Count of Chambord.

Venus. A character in *Tannhäuser*; soprano. Prototype of Holda, a goddess in Teutonic mythology, who personified the power that controlled the productive forces of the earth. Act 1, scene 2; Act 3, scene 3. Rôle created by Schröder-Devrient.

Victors, The. A drama sketched by Wagner at Zürich, under the date of May 16, 1856. The hero, Ananda, an absolutely pure man, renounces sexual love. He is passionately beloved by Prakriti, the beautiful daughter of King Tchandala. The heroine, after vainly suffering the torments of unrequited passion, renounces love, and is received into the order of Buddha by Ananda.

Vienna Opera House, The. P.W. 3. Published as separate pamphlet at the end of Oct. 1863, after publication in the Viennese *Botschafter.*

Villot, Frédéric. Keeper of the imperial museums in Paris; friend and visitor of Wagner.

Virtuoso and the Artist, The. See German Musician in Paris, A. No. 5.

Vivisection, On. P.W. 6. An open letter to Herr Ernst von Weber, author of *The Torture-Chambers of Science.* Published in the *Bayreuther Blätter* Oct. 1879.

Vogelgesang, Kunz. One of the mastersingers in *Die Meistersinger*; tenor. A furrier. Acts 1, 3. Rôle created by Heinrich.

Vogelweide, Walther von der. See Walther von der Vogelweide.

Vogl, Heinrich. Eminent Wagnerian tenor. Born Jan. 15, 1845 at Au, near Munich. Early in life a schoolmaster, received lessons in singing from Franz Lachner. Made his debut Nov. 5, 1865 at the Royal Theatre, Munich, as Max in *Der Freischütz*. Succeeded Schnorr von Carolsfeld as Tristan. Played Loge at the Bayreuth production in 1876. Married Therese Thoma, also an opera singer, who for years was the only Isolde and was the original Sieglinde at Munich. Died at Munich Apr. 21, 1900.

Volsunga Saga. Volsung, son of Rerir, son of Sigi, King of Hunland, son of Odin. Sigmund, son, and Signy, twin-daughter of Volsung. Sigurd (Siegfried) Fafner's-bane, posthumous son of Sigmund.

Saga—story, a tale. The legends and traditions of the Volsung race, beginning with Odin and descending through Sigi and Rerir to Volsung, a great King. Literary product of Iceland, Norway, Sweden and Denmark dating from the 13th century. Many sagas have been translated into German. The writers are unknown. It is believed they were given literary form by priests or monks. Mainly it is a story about one man and usually the elements are insult, killing and revenge. Volsunga saga based on Old Norse poems and their sources relate back to the great migrations of the fifth century, mingling fights and myths of German tribes.

Siegfried (Sigurd). Hero of poems in the *Elder Edda*, also of prose *Volsunga Saga*. According to legend he was son of Sigmundr (Siegmund), a King of the Netherlands.

"According to the Scandinavian story Sigmundr was slain in battle before the birth of Sigurd, but the German story makes him survive his son. Sigurd acquired great fame and riches by slaying the dragon Fafner, but the chief interest of the story centers in his connection with the court of the Burgundian King Gunnar (Gunther). He married Gudrun (Kriemhild), the sister of that king, and won for him by a stratagem the hand of the Valkyrie Brynhild, with whom he had himself previously exchanged vows of love. A quarrel arose between Brynhild and Gudrun, in the course of which the former learnt of the deception which had been practiced upon her and this led eventually to the murder of Sigurd. According to the Scandinavian version he was slain by his brother-in-law Guttorm; according to the German version by the knight Hagen. Gunnar's brothers were subsequently slain while visiting Atli (Etzel), or Attila, King of the Huns, who married Gudrun, after Sigurd's death. According to the German story they were killed at the instigation of Kriemhild in revenge for Siegfried. The Scandinavian version attributes the deed to Atli's lust for gold.

"The story of Sigurd is of German rather than Scandinavian origin, and has given rise to more discussion than any other subject connected with the Teutonic heroic age. Like Achilles he is represented as the perfect embodiment of the ideals of the race, and, as in the case of the Greek hero, it is customary to regard his personality and exploits as mythical. There is no question, however, that the Burgundian king who is said to have been his brother-in-law was an historical person who was slain by the Huns, at the time when the Burgundian kingdom was overthrown by the latter. Sigurd himself is not mentioned by any contemporary writer; but, apart from the dragon incident, there is nothing in the story which affords sufficient justification for regarding his personality as mythical. Opinions, however, vary widely as to the precise proportions of history and fiction which the story contains. The story of Siegfried in Richard Wagner's famous opera-cycle *Der Ring des Nibelungen* is mainly taken from the northern version; but many features, especially the characterization of Hagen, are borrowed from the German story as is also the episode of Siegfried's murder in the forest."

ENCYCLOPAEDIA BRITANNICA (*14th ed. 1929*)
Vol. 20, p. 646.

The prose of the Volsunga Saga was composed probably some time in the 12th century from floating traditions and from songs.

A book on this subject was found by Wagner about Nov. 3, 1848 in the Dresden Royal Library, called *Die Wölsunga-saga*—translated by H. von der Hagen from the old Norse. Wagner says it was published by Hagen about 1812 to 1816.

For an exhaustive treatment of myth and legend connected with *The Ring* trilogy see Dr. Ernst Meinck's *Legendary Bases* (in German), published by Emil Felber, Berlin, 1892: *Die sagenwissenschaftlichen Grundlagen der Nibelungendichtung Richard Wagner's.* Also Miss Jessie L. Weston's *Legends of the Wagner Drama,* London: David Nutt, 1896 (1903).

W

Wälse. Name taken by Wotan when adventuring forth as a hero.

Wagenseil, Johann Christoph. Author of *Nürnberger Chronik* (1697), one of the sources of *Die Meistersinger.* Doctor and Professor of Law. Born at Nuremberg in 1633; died at Altdorf in 1708. His book is an account of the city of Nuremberg and contains a description of the "Master-singers' gracious art."

Wagner, (Gottlob Heinrich) Adolf. (Nov. 14, 1774-Aug. 1, 1835) Brother of Carl Friedrich Wagner, Richard Wagner's father. Educated at the Leipzig Thoma. Entered at 18 for the Theologia Faculty at the Leipzig University. He was a very learned man and a voluminous writer of essays on the Greek poets and of novels and comedies. Author of *Biographien der Reformatoren* and *Zwei Epochen der Modernen Poesie,* the latter a comparison of Dante, Petrarch and Boccaccio on the one hand, with Goethe, Schiller and Wieland on the other. He contributed to the first edition of Brockhaus' *Encyclopedia*. He translated numerous works from Sophocles and Caesar to Lange's *History of Painting*. Author of a celebrated complete edition of the works of Giordano Bruno in the original Latin and Italian. Edited the Italian classics under the title *Parnasso Italiano*. The first complete edition of the poems of Robert Burns in English is his work. His *Theatre und Publikum* may have influenced Richard Wagner's protest against the disgraceful state of modern art at that time. Married Sophie Wendt Oct. 18, 1824.

For a list of his writings and translations see Österlein's *Wagner Katalog* III, 438-9; also Glasenapp's biographic sketch in the *Bayreuther Blätter*, 1885, p. 197-223.

Wagner, (Carl) Albert. (March 2, 1799-Oct. 31, 1874) Eldest son of Carl Friedrich Wagner and brother of Richard. An actor and singer, possessing a very high brilliant tenor voice; stage manager in Berlin and at Würzburg. Leading tenor at Breslau. Married Elise Gollmann in the period of 1827-29, a singer with a great range of voice, a native of Mannheim. A daughter was born to them named Johanna, an eminent soprano, the original Elizabeth in *Tannhäuser* at the age of 17.

Wagner, Anna Dorothea. Daughter of Emanuel Wagner. Wife of John Müller of Altenburg, a master-tailor. Born 1700 (?) at Colmen.

Wagner, Carl Friedrich Wilhelm. (1770-1813) Father of Richard. Born June 17 or 18, 1770 at Leipzig. A clerk of police (actuary) at Leipzig. Attended the University of Leipzig. He was a patron of the theatre, an amateur actor, and supported the Leipzig "privileged" theatre. He had a taste for verse. Married in 1798 Johanna Rosina Bertz (or

Pätz) of Weissenfels. A linguist of ability. In consequence he was used by Marshal Davoust under Napoleon to organize the police when the French army occupied Leipzig. Died Nov. 22, 1813, six months after the birth of his son Richard. Death was due to an epidemic fever arising from dead bodies around the city after the battles on Oct. 18 and 19, 1813. Children, Carl Albert, Carl Gustav, Johanna Rosalie, Carl Julius, Luise Constanze, Clara Wilhelmine, Maria Theresia, Wilhelmine Ottilie and Wilhelm Richard.

Wagner, Carl Gustav. (July 21, 1801-Nov. 12, 1802) Second son of Carl Friedrich Wagner; brother of Richard.

Wagner, Carl Julius. (Aug. 7, 1804-Mar. 29, 1862) Third son of Carl Friedrich Wagner; brother of Richard. Apprenticed to Ludwig Geyer's younger brother, Karl Friedrich Wilhelm, a goldsmith at Eisleben. Died at Dresden.

Wagner, Clara Wilhelmine. (Nov. 29, 1807-Mar. 17, 1875) Sister of Richard. A singer. Married Heinrich Wolfram of Magdeburg, an opera singer. Took a child's part in *Der Bethlehemitische Kindermord* in 1821. Made her début at the Italian Opera in Dresden May 1, 1824 as Angiolina in Rossini's *La Cenerentola.*

Wagner, Cosima. Wife of Richard. Born in Bellagio on Lake Como, Italy, Dec. 24, 1837. Younger daughter of Franz Liszt and the Countesse Marie d'Agoult. Married in 1857 to Hans von Bülow but the marriage was annulled July 18, 1870. Married Richard Wagner August 25, 1870. She had already borne Isolde, Eva and Siegfried. Moved to Bayreuth in 1872. Since Wagner's death in 1883 she became the leading spirit of Bayreuth and developed the annual festival into a world affair. Died in Villa Wahnfried April 1, 1930, in her 93rd year. Buried in the tomb of Richard Wagner in the park of the Villa Wahnfried. Her birth has generally been believed to have occurred on Christmas Day, 1837, but according to the researches of Mary Tibaldi-Chiesa, Italian musicologist, the correct date is Christmas Eve. The birth certificate, found in the Como Cathedral, reads:

"Francesca Gaetana Cosima Liszt, illegittima, nata il 24 dicembre, 1837, battezzata il 26 dal Coadiutore Sac. Pietro Cavadini, da Caterina de Flavigny, abitante all' albergo dell' Angelo in Como al n. 614, e da Francesco Liszt esse pure nello stesso albergo, cattolici, professore di musica il padre e possidente e nobile la madre."

Translated:

Frances Gaetana Cosima Liszt, illegitimate, born on the 24 of December 1837, baptized on the 26 by the Coadjutor, Father Pietro Cavadini, of Caterina de Flavigny, living at the Inn of Angelo in Como no. 614, and Francis Liszt also living at the same inn, catholics; the father, a professor of music, and the mother, of noble birth and well to do .

Wagner, Emmanuel. Eldest son of Samuel Wagner. Born in August, 1664, died 1726 at Kühren. Schoolmaster at Colmen (Kulm) near Thalnitz. Married at Kühren in 1688 Anna Benewitz, eighteen years of age, daughter of schoolmaster and tax-gatherer Ernst Benewitz. Daughter, Anna Dorothea; second daughter, Marie Sophia, born Mar. 19, 1709. Removed about 1702 from Colmen to Kühren to assume the mastership of a school. First son, Samuel Wagner, born at Kühren on Jan. 14, 1703.

Wagner, Eva. Daughter of Richard and Cosima. Born Feb. 17, 1867 in Triebschen, on the Lucerne. Married Houston Stewart Chamberlain at Bayreuth on Dec. 26, 1908.

Wagner, Franziska. (Aug. 28, 1829-June 20, 1895) Daughter of Albert and Elise (Gollmann) Wagner.

154

Niece of Richard Wagner. Married the composer Alexander Ritter, brother of Karl Ritter.

Wagner, Friedlind. Second son of Siegfried Wagner. Born March 29, 1918 at Bayreuth.

Wagner, Gottlob Friedrich. Fourth child and eldest son of Samuel Wagner III. Born at Müglenz on Feb. 18, 1736. Father of Carl Friedrich Wilhelm Wagner and grandfather of Richard Wagner. Probably educated at the Thoma School in Leipzig. Student of theology at the Leipzig University, entered Mar. 16, 1759. Later, Receiver of Taxes for the Electoral Excise at Leipzig. Married 1769, in the Schönefeld parish church, Sophia Eichel, only daughter of Gottlob Friedrich Eichel, who conducted a charity school. Died Mar. 21, 1795.

Wagner, Isolde. Daughter of Richard and Cosima Wagner. Born April 12, 1865. Von Bülow believed the child to be his own, and Wagner made himself its godfather. She was really Wagner's child, however. Married Franz Beidler.

Wagner, Johanna. Niece of Richard Wagner. Born at Hanover, Oct. 13, 1828. Daughter of Albert Wagner who married Elise Gollmann. She had a voice of abnormal compass—three octaves and two notes. Richard Wagner and Albert lived together in Würzburg during 1833. Johanna, then five years old, sang everything she heard. Appeared at six as Salome in the *Donauweibschen*. Richard Wagner obtained in 1844 a temporary engagement for her at the Royal Opera at Dresden. She sang with success parts of Irma in *Maurer und Schlosser* when sixteen and Agathe in *Der Freischütz*. She created the part of Elizabeth when seventeen, appearing in *Tannhäuser* Oct. 21, 1845.

Appeared as Norma, singing in Italian. Her répertoire included Fidelio, Valentine, Adriano, Susanna, Reiza, Favorita, Donna Anna, Recha, Euryanthe, Ernani, Sextus, Weisse Dame, etc. Sang Fidès in the first German production of *Le Prophète*. Permanently engaged in 1850 at the Royal Opera House in Berlin. Appeared in London in 1856 as Tancredi, Lucrezia Borgia and Romeo. Married in 1859 Herr Landrath Jachmann. Lost her voice completely two years later. Then entered upon a career as actress. Sang at Bayreuth on May 22, 1872, in a performance of Beethoven's *Ninth Symphony*, solo alto part. In 1876 at the opening of the Wagner Theatre at Bayreuth, she took minor parts of Schwertleite and first Norn. Accepted in 1882 the position of professorship of dramatic singing in the Royal School of Music in Munich "in the hope of training young artists in the spirit and traditions of her uncle, to be worthy interpreters of his works." Retired in 1884 and went to live in Berlin. Died at Würzburg Oct. 16, 1894.

Wagner, Johanna Rosalie. (Mar. 4, 1803-Oct. 12, 1837) Eldest daughter of Carl Friedrich. Sister of Richard Wagner; an actress. Leading actress at the Leipzig theatre. Married Dr. Gotthard Oswald Marbach, a tutor of philosophy and physics at the University of Liepzig, on Oct. 24, 1836 at Schönefeld. Appeared March 2, 1818 in Dresden, in *Das Erntefest*, a drama written by her step-father, Ludwig Geyer. Oct. 7, 1837 she gave birth to a daughter, Margarethe Johanna Rosalie, and five days later died.

Wagner, Johanna Rosina (Bertz or Pätz). (Sept. 19, 1779-1848) Mother of Richard Wagner. A native of Weissenfels. Married Carl Friedrich Wilhelm Wagner June 2, 1798. She was a small, active woman; self-possessed, witty, of a good disposition, with a large amount of common sense, thrifty and of a very affectionate nature. According to Mrs. Burrell the real maiden name of Wagner's mother was Pätz.

Wagner, Luise Constanze. (Dec. 14, 1805-Jan. 2, 1872) Sister of Richard, and second daughter of Carl Friedrich Wagner. An actress. Married Friedrich Brockhaus, a Leipzig publisher, June 16, 1828. Appeared in 1814 in *Das Mädchen aus der Fremde*, a comedy by Ludwig Geyer.

Wagner, Maria Theresia. (Apr. 1, 1809-Jan. 1814) Fourth daughter of Carl Friedrich Wagner; sister of Richard.

Wagner, Marie. (Jan. 25, 1831-May 19, 1876) Daughter of Albert and Elise (Gollmann) Wagner; niece of Richard Wagner. Married Carl Jacoby.

Wagner, Minna. See Planer, Christine Wilhelmine.

Wagner, (Wilhelm) Richard. (May 22, 1813-Feb. 13, 1883)

ANCESTRY

Samuel (1643-1705), Emmanuel (1664-1726), Samuel, the younger (1703-1750), Gottlob Friedrich (1736-1795), Carl Friedrich Wilhelm (1770-1813). His ancestors were natives of Saxony, fairly well educated and fairly well-to-do. The last-named was a clerk of police (actuary) at Leipzig. Mother, Johanna Bertz (See Wagner, Johanna Rosina). According to Ernest Newman it is not definitely known whether Richard was the son of Carl Friedrich Wagner or of Ludwig Geyer, although Wagner himself had expressed the idea that Geyer might be his real father. However in his autobiography Wagner says that Friedrich Wagner was his father.

WAG

Early Years

Born May 22, 1813, at Leipzig in "The House of the White and Red Lion," No. 22 House Brühl. (See Leipzig) The youngest of nine children, the others being Carl Albert, Carl Gustav, Johanna Rosalie, Carl Julius, Luise Constanze, Clara Wilhelmine, Maria Theresia, and Wilhelmine Ottilie.

He attended a private school at Eisleben when eight years old, living with a brother of Ludwig Geyer, his step-father. In Dec. 1822 he entered the Dresden Kreuzschule under the name of Wilhelm Richard Geyer, taking the name of his step-father, his own father having died Nov. 22, 1813. Remained there five years. In *Mein Leben* [1] he says that he conceived a profound love for the classicism of Homer and out of school hours translated the first twelve books of the Odyssey. Revelled in mythology. At eleven resolved to become a poet and planned vast tragedies. Delved into Shakespeare and translated a speech of Romeo into metrical German. For two years worked on a grand tragedy composed of elements from *Hamlet* and *King Lear*. Loved the piano, although he never learned to play it. Drummed out *Der Frei-schütz* by ear. Watched Weber pass his house with religious awe—the composer became his idol. Returned with his family to Leipzig in 1827 and entered the Nicolaischule the following year. First heard the works of Beethoven at the concerts of the Leipzig Gewandhaus. Studied a borrowed copy of Logier's treatise on harmony and counterpoint and tried to master it in a week. Gottlieb Müller, afterward organist at Altenburg, was engaged as his music teacher. Studied under Theodor Weinlig, cantor of the Thomas School which he attended in 1830. Influ-

[1] My Life. English translation published by Dodd, Mead & Co., New York, 1911.

enced greatly by the marvellous incidents in the stories of Ernst Theodor Hoffmann, then recently dead and at the height of his fame in Germany.

Entered the University of Leipzig Feb. 23, 1831, mainly to hear lectures on aesthetics and philosophy.

EARLY WORKS

In 1831 he wrote a piano sonata, Opus 1, followed by a Polonaise in D for four hands, Opus 2; a fantasie in F sharp minor for piano; and two overtures. In 1832 wrote a symphony in C major, as well as at Prague a libretto for a tragic opera, *Die Hochzeit* (The Wedding). Secured a position as chorus-master at the Würzburg Theatre and composed there another opera, *Die Feen*, in 1833. At Teplitz in 1834 sketched his next opera, *Das Liebesverbot*. In August, 1834 made a sketch of a second symphony which was discovered in 1886 by W. Tappert. It is in E major and Tappert's article may be found, with musical illustrations, in the *Musikalisches Wochenblatt* for Sept. 30 and Oct. 7, 1886.

Became conductor in a small operatic theatre in Magdeburg in 1834. Married Minna (Wilhelmine) Planer on Nov. 24, 1836 at Königsberg. Musical director at the Königsberg Theatre in January 1837. At Königsberg he wrote the overture *Rule Britannia*, also about this time an overture entitled *Polonia*. Appointed director of music in the theatre at Riga where his wife and her sister, Theresa Planer, were also engaged for the comedy performances. He lived in a house in the outskirts of the town. Conducted ten orchestral concerts. Began to write a comic opera entitled *Die Glückliche Bärenfamilie* (The Happy Bear Family) which was left unfinished.

Later Works

He took passage with his wife on a small sailing ship in 1839, the "Thetis," for London, going thence to Paris via Boulogne where he met Meyerbeer. Arrived in Paris September 1839 and remained there till April 7, 1842. Letters from Meyerbeer introduced him to men in Paris who helped him. Composed several songs and worked at his *Rienzi*. Here he met Liszt. He moved to Meudon, a suburb, and back to Paris. At Meudon he wrote *The Flying Dutchman*. Left Paris Apr. 7, 1842 for Dresden, where he secured the post of Hofkapellmeister in the Dresden Theatre, and was made conductor of the Liedertafel and of the Sangerfest. Went to Marienbad in 1844 where he made first drafts of *Die Meistersinger* and *Lohengrin*. Engaged in revolutionary proceedings in Saxony, 1848-49, which, proving unsuccessful, led to his removal to Weimar where he was befriended by Liszt. Thence he proceeded to Zürich. Then to Paris in 1849, returning to Zürich in July. Started composing his *Ring of the Nibelungs*, first called *Siegfried's Tod*, consisting of *Das Rheingold, Die Walküre, Siegfried* and *Götterdämmerung*. Went to London in 1855 to preside over the Old London Philharmonic concerts. Resided at 22 Portland Terrace, Regent's Park. Returned to Zürich via Paris. Started work on *Tristan und Isolde*. Went to Paris on a fruitless errand to arrange for a performance of *Rienzi*. Back again to Zürich. Thence to Venice and shortly afterward returned to Switzerland, residing on the shores of Lake Lucerne. There he completed *Tristan*. Wagner left Zürich suddenly and finally on Aug. 17, 1859. Went to Geneva, en route for Paris. Arrived in Paris in Sept. 1859. Gave there three concerts in the Théâtre des Italiens in 1860. *Tannhäuser* was performed at the Grand

Opera by order of Emperor Napoleon III. The performance was spoiled by members of the Jockey Club who drowned the music by the blowing of hunting whistles. Wagner went to Vienna where, on May 15, 1861, for the first time he heard his opera *Lohengrin*. Undertook a concert tour in 1862, visiting Carlsruhe, Prague and Weimar, and went into Russia. Minna left him in 1861 and went to Leipzig to live with her relatives. Here she died in 1866. Wagner went to Zürich, residing with an old friend, Mme. Wille. He went to Stuttgart to arrange for performance of his operas. There a messenger from the youthful King of Bavaria found him and took him to Munich where he found rest and help under the royal patronage. A special theatre was projected for him at Munich but, owing to false rumors as to the cost stirring up opposition, it was not erected. He left Munich in Dec. 1865 for Vevay and Geneva, Switzerland. In Feb. 1866 he stayed at Triebschen, near Lucerne, whence he removed in 1872 to Bayreuth.

Married Cosima Liszt, divorced wife of Hans von Bülow, on Aug. 25, 1870. Composed *Siegfried Idyll* in 1871. Published in 1870 *On Conducting* and *Beethoven*. In 1871 he wrote *Kaisermarsch*. Went to Bayreuth to live in April 1872. Resided at first in the village of Donndorf, an hour's ride from Bayreuth. In 1874 was located in the Villa Wahnfried, built for him, in Bayreuth. Under his direction a special theatre, the Festspielhaus, was erected at Bayreuth in 1872-76, q.v. He went to Italy for a rest. Then to London in 1877 where he and Hans Richter jointly conducted concerts to raise money needed to meet a deficit of $37,000 in the erection of the Festspielhaus. Returned to Italy in 1879 in search of relief from erysipelas. Returned to Bayreuth in May 1882. After the first performance of *Parsifal* he

WAG

went to Venice, residing in the Vendramini Palace on the Grand Canal. There he died on Feb. 13, 1883. His body was brought to Bayreuth and after public funeral ceremonies was buried at Wahnfried.

A sketch of his life was prepared by Wagner at the request of his friend Laube and was published in the *Zeitung für die Elegante Welt*. An English translation is in Burlingame's *Wagner's Art Life and Theories*,[1] and a French version in Benoit's *R. Wagner Souvenirs*.

PERSONAL APPEARANCE AND CHARACTERISTICS

The warrant issued by the Dresden police is translated from Kastner's *Wagner Katalog* as follows:

"The royal Kapellmeister, Richard Wagner, of this city, described below, is to be placed under trial for active participation in the riots which have taken place here, but has not been found so far. All police districts are accordingly notified and requested to arrest Wagner on sight and notify us accordingly. Dresden, May 16, 1849.

The City Police Deputation
v. Oppel."

"Wagner is thirty-seven to thirty-eight years of age, of medium stature, has brown hair, an open forehead; eyebrows, brown; eyes, grayish blue; nose and mouth, proportioned; chin, round, and wears spectacles. Special characteristics: rapid in movements and speech. Dress: coat of dark green buckskin, trousers of black cloth, velvet vest; silk neckerchief, ordinary felt hat and boots."

Praeger, in *Wagner as I Knew Him*,[2] says:

"In stature Wagner was below the middle size, and like most undersized men always held himself strictly erect. He had an unusually wiry, muscular frame, small feet, an aristocratic feature which did not extend to his hands. It was his head, however, that could not fail to strike even the least inquiring that there he had to do with no ordinary mortal. The development of the frontal part, which a phrenologist would class at a glance amongst those belonging only to the masterminds, impressed every one. His eyes had a piercing power,

[1] See Bibliography.
[2] Longmans, Green & Co. New York, 1892.

162

but were kindly withal, and were ready to smile at a witty remark. Richard Wagner lacked eyebrows, but nature, as if to make up for this deficiency, bestowed on him a most abundant crop of bushy hair which he carefully kept brushed back, thereby exposing the whole of his really Jupiter-like brow. His mouth was very small. He had thin lips and small teeth, signs of a determined character. The nose was large and in after life somewhat disfigured by the early-acquired habit of snuff-taking. The back of his head was fully developed. These were according to phrenological principles power and energy. Its shape was very similar to that of Luther, with whom, indeed, he had more than one point of character in common."

"As a boy he was passionate and strong-headed. His violent temper and obstinate determination were not to be thwarted in anything he had set his mind to. Among boys such wilfulness of character was the cause of frequent dissensions. He rarely, however, came to blows, for he had a shrewd wit and was winningly entreating in speech, and with much adroitness would bend them to his whims.

"Erysipelas sorely tried the boy during his school life. Every change in the weather was a trouble to him. As regards the loss of his eyebrows, an affliction which ever caused him some regret, Wagner attributed it to a violent attack of St. Anthony fire, as this painful malady is also called."

In a passport dated May 30, 1849 he is described as

"Musical composer, of Leipzig; 36 years old; 5 ft. 5-½ in. high; hair brown, eyebrows brown, eyes blue; nose medium, mouth medium, chin round."

See Wille, Elisa (Slomann).

A chronological table and a summary view of Richard Wagner's Life is in Chamberlain's *Richard Wagner*; Phila. J. B. Lippincott Co. 1900, p. 106-10.

Wagner, Samuel (I). First known ancestor of Richard Wagner. A schoolmaster of Thammenhain near Wurzen in the Liepzig district near the Prussian frontier but formerly in mid-Saxony. Born 1643, died 1705. Married Barbara ——, who died 1701. Son, Emmanuel Wagner. Married his second wife, Anna, 1703, who died 1718.

163

Wagner, Samuel (II). Second son of Samuel (I). Born Oct. 29, 1676. Died Sept. 8, 1709. Schoolmaster at Gross-Zschepa. Later, took his father's place as schoolmaster and organist at Thammenhain. His eldest son, Hans Samuel born in May, 1705. Died Jan. 14, 1706.

Wagner, Samuel (III) (the younger). Born 1703, died Nov. 22, 1750. Son of Emmanuel Wagner. Organist, cantor and schoolmaster at Müglenz near Wurzen. Married 1728 Anna Sophia Rössig of Dahlen. Daughters, Johanna Sophie, Christine Eleonore and Susanna Caroline. Sons, Gottlob Friedrich and Samuel August.

Wagner, Samuel August. Second son of Samuel Wagner III. Born Aug. 13, 1745, at Müglenz.

Wagner, Siegfried (Helferich Siegfried Richard). Son of Richard Wagner and Cosima von Bülow. Born June 6, 1869 at Triebschen. A musician and composer. He studied to be an architect and did design the monument to his grandfather, Liszt, at Bayreuth. Studied music, however, under Humperdinck and Kniese. Acted as sub-conductor at Bayreuth in 1894 and subsequently. His compositions are as follows:

Symphonic poem—*Sehnsucht*; performed in 1895.

OPERAS

Der Bärenhäuter; performed at Munich in 1899.
Herzog Wildfang; performed at Munich in 1901.
Der Kobold; 1904, performed at Hamburg, 1905.
Also:

Bruder Lustig, 1905.
Sternengebot, 1908.
Banadietrich, 1910.
Schwarzschwanenreich, 1918.

Sonnenflammen, 1918.
Der Friedensengel, 1915.
Der Heidenkönig, 1915.
An allem ist Hütchen schuld, 1917.
Der Schmeid von Marienberg, 1920.
Konzertstück, for flute and small orchestra, 1913.
Violin Concerto, 1915.
Choral work *Der Fahnen-schwur*, 1914.

Married Winifred Williams. He came to America in 1924 for a concert tour, to raise funds for the Wagnerian festival, and was successful. Died at the Municipal Hospital, Bayreuth, Aug. 4, 1930 of heart trouble, during the festival. Buried in the city cemetery.

Wagner, Verena. Daughter of Siegfried Wagner. Born Dec. 2, 1920 in Bayreuth.

Wagner, Wieland. Son of Siegfried Wagner. Born in Bayreuth Jan. 5, 1917. Is gifted musically with especial talent for plays. He has, among other things, designed the new *Parsifal* stage-settings used for the first time in 1937 at Bayreuth. He is a prominent photographer.

Wagner, Wilhelmine Ottilie. (Mar. 14, 1811-Mar. 17, 1883) Fifth daughter of Carl Friedrich Wagner; sister of Richard. Married Dr. Hermann Brockhaus Apr. 11, 1836, a brilliant Sanscrit scholar, at the Church of St. Nicholas in Dresden.

Wagner, Winifred (Williams). Wife of Siegfried Wagner. Born June 23, 1897 in Hastings, Sussex County, England. Her father was an author. She lost her parents very early in life and was adopted by Karl Klindworth, the celebrated pianist and arranger of Chopin's and Wagner's works.

Wagner, Wolfgang. Third son of Siegfried Wagner. Born Aug. 30, 1919 in Bayreuth. He has a pronounced gift for the technical part of acting and is also a good photographer.

Wagner Lexikon. A collection of criticisms against Wagner compiled by Tappert in a pamphlet of 48 pages.

Wagner Societies. Plan conceived by Emil Heckel, music publisher of Mannheim, who organized one in Mannheim in June 1871, to provide funds for building the Festspielhaus at Bayreuth. The society plan spread and similar organizations were formed in leading cities in Europe and America. Each member was to pay five florins, which entitled him to one chance in a patron's certificate, one of which was bought for each 35 members. The society was also to give concerts and to use the proceeds in the purchase of certificates. At a gathering of delegates in Munich in 1877 one general association was formed with headquarters in Bayreuth.

The London Wagner Society was founded by Mr. Edward Dannreuther who was Wagner's host in 1877. He is the author of an essay on Wagner in Grove's *Dictionary of Music and Musicians.*

See Bayreuth; Bayreuther Blätter.

Wahn! wahn! "Mad, mad, all the world mad!" Famous monologue of Hans Sachs in *Die Meistersinger*, Act 3.

Wahnfried ("fancies at peace.") A villa built for Wagner at Bayreuth in 1874, where his widow lived until her death in 1930. It has a fresco over the door with four figures—Wotan, as representative of Germany mythology, two females symbolizing Music and Tragedy, and the boy Siegfried indicating the music-drama of the future. These figures bear the likenesses of Betz, Cosima Wagner, Schröder-Devrient, and Siegfried Wagner. Beneath the figures are three tablets, with the words: "Hier wo mein Wähnen Frieden fand Wahnfried sei dieses Haus von mir benannt." (Here where my fancies came to rest, Wahnfried be this house christened.)

"We pass through the door into a large hall, the ceiling of which is the roof itself, whence light is admitted through a colored glass window. Above we see a gallery leading to the family- and bed-rooms. On the right below is the dining-room, on the left the spacious library and reception-room. This room is elegantly adorned with the savings of a lifetime, the trophies of various triumphs. The music shelves and book-shelves are filled with the volumes of Wagner's favorite authors and composers, historic and philosophic books, orchestral and operatic scores. The walls are adorned with portraits of his mother and stepfather, Ludwig Geyer, Beethoven, Schopen-hauer, King Ludwig, Schiller and Goethe, Liszt and his daughter Cosima. In one corner of the room is the magnificent Steinway Grand which served to convince Wagner that in one branch of music, at any rate, America leads the world. In front of the house is a bronze statue of Ludwig II, and the grounds are further adorned with trees and shrubbery, which at present almost conceal the house from the street."

FINCK, *Vol. II, p. 270.*[1]

"Wagner's rooms are still partly preserved as he left them in 1882. They are furnished in perfect taste, and contain an almost overwhelming array of art treasures, previous memen-toes. In the shaded garden, which adjoins the Hofgarten, a simple granite slab marks the spot where Richard Wagner and, later, Cosima Wagner, found a last resting place."

From a pamphlet issued by the STÄDTISCHES VERKEHRSAMT, *Bayreuth.*

Original manuscripts of Wagner's works and writings are preserved in the archives and the memorial room.

Waiting (L'Attente). Listed in Musical Works— Songs. "Sleep, My Child." Words by Victor Hugo. Paris 1839-40. Appeared as a musical supplement to Lewald's *Europa*, 1841 and 1842. Republished with a German translation 1871.

[1] Wagner and his works. C. Scribner's Sons, New York, 1907.

Waldweben. Forest-murmurs tone-poem in *Siegfried*, Act 2, in which the orchestra imitates the weaving of the forest leaves and shadows.

Walhalla. Castle of refuge of the gods and goddesses in *The Ring*.

Walküre, Die. See Ring of the Nibelungs, The; The Valkyries.

Walkyrs, The. See Valkyries, The.

Walther von der Vogelweide. A character in *Tannhäuser*; tenor. A poet and contemporary of Wolfram von Eschenbach. A native of Tyrol and a lyric singer. He lived near Würzburg. Act 1, scene 4; Act 2, scene 4. Rôle created by Schloss.

Walther von Stolzing. A character in *Die Meistersinger*; tenor. A young Franconian knight. Acts 1, 2, 3. Rôle created by Nachbaur.

Waltraute. A character in *The Ring*; mezzo-soprano. a walkyr or valkyrie. Sister of Brünnhilde.
Die Walküre, Act 3. Rôle created at first Festspielhaus performance by Luise Jäide.
Götterdämmerung, Act 1. Rôle created by Luise Jäide.

Wanderer, The. A character in *The Ring*; baritone-bass. Wotan. *Siegfried*, Acts 1, 2, 3. Rôle created by Franz Betz.

Wartburg. A famous hill in the Thuringian valley of Germany. Here in the 13th century the Landgrave Hermann of Thuringia held contests of song—not of musicians but of poets. Wagner gave to one of the ridges the name of Hörselberg, the legendary location of the meetings between Tannhäuser and Venus.

"The interior was regarded as one of the principal seats of the Old-German Holda, the kind and gracious goddess whose yearly progress through the land brought thrift and fruitfulness to field and meadow." (R.W.)

In *Tannhäuser* it is named the Venusberg.

Was ist deutsch? See What is German?

Was nuetzt diese Erkenntniss? See Religion and Art, No. 1: What Boots this Knowledge?

Weber, Carl Maria Friedrich Ernest Freiherr von. Composer of *Der Freischütz*, the music of which fascinated Richard Wagner in his early years. "When Weber passed our house," says Wagner, "I used to watch him with something akin to religious awe." Born 1786 in Eutin. Died in London June 4, 1826.

> See Report on the home-bringing of the mortal remains of Karl Maria von Weber; Speech at Weber's last resting place; Musical Works; Weber's Grabe, An.

Weber's Grabe, An (At Weber's Grave).
  (a) Traversmarsch (Funeral March) for wind instruments on motives from Euryanthe;
  (b) Double quartet for voices.
       Composed in 1844 and performed on Dec. 15 of that year. Score published in 1872.

Weibliche im Menschlichen, Über das. See Human Womanly, The.

Weimar. Wagner escaped from Dresden in 1849 and proceeded to Weimar where he was under the protection of Liszt. Here was first produced the opera *Lohengrin*.

Weinlig, Theodor. (1780-1842) Cantor at St. Thomas's Church, Leipzig from 1823, under whom Wagner studied counterpoint. Died in March 1842.

169

Wellgunde. A character in *The Ring*; soprano. A
Rhinemaiden.

> *Das Rheingold,* Scenes 1, 4. Rôle created by
> Frau Vogel.
> *Götterdämmerung,* Act 3. Rôle created by Marie
> Lehmann.

Wesendonck, Mathilde (Luckemeyer). Born at
Elberfeld Dec. 23, 1828. Parents, Karl Luckemeyer
and Johanna (Stein). Married Otto May 19, 1848;
his second wife.
See Wesendoncks, The.

Wesendonck, Otto. Born at Elberfeld Mar. 16, 1815.
Married first in October 1844. Married Mathilde
Luckemeyer, his second wife, May 19, 1848. Of
Netherlands descent. His pedigree dates back to the
15th century. At 18 he went to the United States.
He became the European representative of the New
York import firm of Löschigk, Wesendonck & Co.
Died November 1896.
See Wesendoncks, The.

Wesendoncks, The. Otto was a retired merchant
of wealth, a music-lover and admirer of Wagner, and
a friend of his in Zürich. His wife's (Mathilde's)
society was sought by Wagner, which aroused the
jealousy of Minna. An open break occurred in 1856.
To Mrs. Wesendonck was dedicated a sonata and the
prelude to *Die Walküre.* She was his friend and
confidante. The whole affair is discussed in *Richard
Wagner in Zürich* by M. Belart, published in Leipzig
in 1900. The Wesendoncks had a villa in Mariafeld
near Zürich.

"As there never could be talk between us of a union, our
deep attachment took that wistful character which holds all

170

base and vulgar thoughts aloof, and discerns its only source of gladness in the welfare of each other."

> *Letter of Richard Wagner to his sister Clara Wolfram Aug. 20, 1858.* RICHARD WAGNER TO MATHILDE WESENDONK, *New York: Chas. Scribner's Sons, 1905.*

Mathilde was born at Elberfeld Dec. 23, 1828. Married Otto May 19, 1848. First met Wagner in February 1852. A son, Paul, was born at Düsseldorf November 1849; died four months later. Lived at the Hotel Baur au Lac at Zürich. Daughter, Myrrha, born at Zürich Aug. 7, 1851. Sons were Guido, born Sept. 13, 1855; Karl, April 18, 1857, and Hans, June 16, 1862. Lived later in a splendid villa which they built in the rural suburb, Enge, "Green Hill," from August 1857 to 1872. Removed to Dresden and in 1882 to Berlin, with a country-seat "Traunblick" on the shores of the Traunsee, Salzkammerget. Here Mathilde died on Aug. 31, 1902 after a brief illness. Her father was a member of the firm of Kutter & Luckemeyer, New York, in the silk trade. She was the author of *Recollections*.

> "She is and stays my first and only love."
> *Richard Wagner to Frau Elisa Wille, June 5, 1863.*
> *Trans. by William Ashton Ellis.*

What Boots this Knowledge? See Religion and Art, No. 1.

What is German? P.W. 4. Written near the end of 1865. Published in the second number of *Bayreuther Blätter* Feb. 1878. Reprinted in Vol. II of *Collected Writings*.

What is the Relation of our Efforts to the Monarchy? A paper by Wagner read before the society of the Fatherland Union.

Wibelungen, The. See Wibelungs, The: World-history as told in Saga.

171

Wibelungs, The: World-history as told in Saga. P.W. 7. An essay by Wagner written in the summer of 1848, published at Leipzig in 1850. Treats of the history of the world according to tradition and shows agreement of history and mythology in various facts.

Wieland. A character in *Wieland the Smith*, brother to Eigel and Helferich.

Wieland the Smith (Wieland der Schmied). Prose sketch of a libretto written by Wagner while at Zürich, 1849-50. A drama in three acts and thirteen scenes. Scene laid in Norway. Liszt declined to compose the music as he had determined never to write a German opera. It was never set to music.

The myth of Wieland Wagner conceived principally as the symbolical representation of true art, which, enslaved by the rudest power, and forced to serve inartistic purposes, in deepest suffering rises to the greatest height of its miraculous strength, and regains freedom and splendour with the destruction of the suppressing powers. (Muncker)

For a fine account in all its aspects see Dr. Rudolph Schlösser's essay in the *Bayreuther Blätter* 1895, p. 30-64.

Wiener hof-Opern-theatre, Das. See Vienna Opera-House, The.

Wille, Elisa (Slomann) (1809-1893). Daughter of a Hamburg ship-owner. Friend of Richard Wagner, becoming acquainted with him in 1843. Lived at Mariafeld, near Zürich. At her home he worked on *Die Meistersinger*.

Frau Wille was a novelist, wife of a Hamburg journalist. She published in the *Deutsche Rundschau* for May and June, 1887 fifteen letters of Wagner.

"The delicate mobile figure, the head with the mighty forehead, the keen eyes, and the energetic traits about his small, firmly closed mouth. An artist who sat next to me, called my attention to the straight, projecting chin, which, as if cut from stone, gave the face a peculiar character. Wagner's wife was of pleasing appearance; she was gay and talkative, and appeared to be especially happy in society. He himself was very animated, self-conscious, but amiable and free from affectation."

Wille, François. A Hamburg journalist, friend of Wagner, with whom for a time he lived. His wife, Frau Elisa Wille, was a novelist and an understanding friend of Wagner.

Winterstürme. See Liebeslied, Siegmund's.

Woglinde. A character in *The Ring*; soprano. A Rhinemaiden.

> *Das Rheingold*, Scenes 1, 4. Rôle created by Fr. Kaufmann.
> *Götterdämmerung*, Act 3. Rôle created by Lilli Lehmann.

Wolfe. Father of Siegmund as told in Siegmund's narrative, *Die Walküre*, Act 1.

Wolfram von Eschenbach. Author of *Parzival*; London, David Nutt. Also a character in *Tannhäuser*; baritone. Act 1, scene 4; Act 2, scenes 2, 4; Act 3, scenes 1, 2, 3. Rôle created by Mitterwürzer.

Wollen wir hoffen? See Shall we hope?

Wolzogen, Baron Hans Paul von. Friend and interpreter of Wagner, playwright, critic and composer. Born in Potsdam, Germany, in 1849 the son of the intendant of the Schwerin court theatre. Educated at the University of Berlin, majoring in comparative philology and mythology. On his wedding trip in 1873 he visited Bayreuth, meeting Wagner, with whose works he was acquainted and which he admired. At Wagner's request he moved in 1877 from Potsdam to Bayreuth in order to edit the *Bayreuther Blätter*, in which post he remained for about half a century. Author of *Thematischer Leitfäden*—

leading motives or thematic guides to *The Ring, Tristan* and *Parsifal*. During the last years of Wagner's life he was closely identified with the master and was generally thought to be the final authority on the later interpreters of the composer. At the Bayreuth Festival of 1931 he acclaimed a performance of *Parsifal*, directed by Arturo Toscanini, as the greatest achievement since that of Levi in 1882. Some of Wolzogen's books were: *Recollections of Wagner, Guide Through Der Ring des Nibelungen* and *Wagner's Spiritual World*. As a composer his works included: Libretti of the operas *Viola D'Amore, Morning, The Castle of Hearts* and *Flauto-Solo*. His play *Longinus* was given at the Weimar Festival in 1926. He was a member of the central committee of the general Richard Wagner Association. He died at Bayreuth June 2, 1938.

Wotan. A character in *The Ring*; baritone-bass. Greatest of the gods. In the original edition of the poem, 1853, the name was spelt Wodan.
> *Das Rheingold*, Scenes 2, 3, 4. Rôle created by Kindermann.
> *Die Walküre*, Acts 2, 3. Rôle created by Kindermann.

Wotan's Farewell. Addressed to Brünnhilde at the close of Act 3, *Die Walküre*.

Würzburg. Here Wagner sought employment as a musician at the Würzburg theatre.

Y

Youthful Symphony, A. P.W. 6. Report on the reperformance of an early work (Symphony in C). Published in *Musikalisches Wochenblatt* 1883. Performed in England, first, at London Symphony Concert Nov. 29, 1887, conductor, Mr. Henschel.

Z

Zorn, Balthazar. One of the mastersingers in *Die Meistersinger*; tenor. A pewterer. Acts 1, 3. Rôle created by Weixlstorfer.

Zum Vortrage der Neunten Symphonie Beethoven's. See Rendering of Beethoven's Ninth Symphony, The.

Zürich. Wagner resided:
1. At Alex. Müller's on the lower Rennweg, "Im Tannenbaum," staying there two months. Today it is the third house from the lower end of the Rennweg. His room overlooked the "Fröschengraben" or Frog's Ditch, changed to Bahnhofstrasse. In that room was written *Art and Revolution*.
2. "Zur Akazie," the Acacia, now No. 7 Ötenbachstrasse, Zürich 1.
3. No. 3 Schanzengraben, Zürich 2.
4. "Hintere Escherhäuser" No. 182, off the Zeltweg, commune of Hottingen. Now No. 3 Steinwiesstrasse.
5. "Vordere Escherhäuser"; now Zeltweg. It bears a memorial tablet. At first he occupied the ground floor left, afterward the third story.
6. On returning from Paris in 1850, the house "Zum Abendstern," now about 22 Sternenstrasse, Zürich 2. His friends dubbed it "Villa Rienzi."
7. Villa Wesendonck on the "Green Hill," Zürich 2, in the park of the Rieter-Bodmer residence, in 1857.

APPENDIX

BIBLIOGRAPHY

ABELL, A. M. Some rare portraits and incidents in the life of Wagner. Musical Courier. 61 :nos. 9, 10, 11, 12, 13. New York. 1910.

BARRY, R. MILNER. Bayreuth and Franconian Switzerland. S. Sonnenschein, Lowrey & Co. London. 1887.

BARTHOU, LOUIS. The prodigious lover. New aspects in the life of Richard Wagner. Translated by Henry Irving Brock. Duffield & Co. New York. 1927.

BEKKER, PAUL. Richard Wagner: his life in his work. Translated by M. M. Bozman. J. M. Dent & Sons. London. 1931.

BROWNELL, GERTRUDE (HALL). The Wagnerian romances. A. A. Knopf. New York. 1925.

BRUNO, GUIDO. Richard Wagner the egoist. Bruno Chap Books. New York. 1915.

BÜLOW, HANS VON. Letters of Hans von Bülow. Translated by Hannah Waller.

BURLINGAME, E. L. Art, life and theories of Richard Wagner. Translations of articles by Wagner. H. Holt & Co. New York. 1875.

BURRELL, MARY. Richard Wagner, his life and works from 1813 to 1834. London. 1898.

CHAMBERLAIN, HOUSTON STEWART. Richard Wagner. Translated by G. Ainslee Hight. J. M. Dent & Sons. London. 1900.

CHAMBERLAIN, HOUSTON STEWART. The Wagnerian Drama. J. Lane. London. 1915.

CORDER, FREDERICK. Wagner. T. C. & E. C. Jack. London. 1912; Frederick A. Stokes Co. New York. 1912.

179

DANNREUTHER, EDWARD. Richard Wagner, his tendencies and theories. London. 1873.

DRY, WAKELING. Wagner. T. N. Foulis. London. 1924.

DU MOULIN-ECKART, COUNT RICHARD. Cosima Wagner. 2 vols. Translated by Catherine Alison Phillips. A. A. Knopf. New York. 1930.

ELLIS, WILLIAM ASHTON. Richard Wagner contra militarism. Musical Times. London. 1915.

ELLIS, WILLIAM ASHTON. Richard Wagner to Mathilde Wesendonck. Scribner. New York. 1905.

ELLIS, WILLIAM ASHTON. Richard Wagner's prose works. Translation. 8 vols. (Gesammelte Schriften, 10 vols.) Kegan Paul, Trench, Trubner & Co. London. 1892-99.

ELLIS, WILLIAM ASHTON. Wagner and latter-day France. Musical Times. London. 1915.

FEHR, MAX. Richard Wagner's Swiss period. Sauerländer & Co. Aarau and Leipzig.

FINCK, HENRY T. Wagner and his works. 2 vols. Scribner. New York. 1907.

FISCHER, GEORGE ALEXANDER. Beethoven, a character study, together with Wagner's indebtedness to Beethoven. Dodd, Mead & Co. New York. 1905.

FÖRSTER-NIETZSCHE, ELIZABETH. Wagner and Nietzsche. Musical Quarterly. New York. 1918.

FROST, WILLIAM HENRY. The Wagner story book. Scribner. New York. 1894-95.

GAUTIER, JUDITH. Richard Wagner and his poetical work from Rienzi to Parsifal. A. Williams & Co. Boston. 1883.

GAUTIER, JUDITH. Wagner at home. Mills & Boon. London. 1910.

GERARD, FRANCES A. Wagner, Bayreuth and the festival plays. Jarrold & Sons. London. 1901.

GLASENAPP, CARL F. Life of Richard Wagner. Translated by William Ashton Ellis. 6 vols. Kegan Paul, Trench, Trubner & Co. London. 1900.

GLASENAPP, CARL F. Wagner Encyclopädie. Fritzch. 1891.

GLASENAPP, CARL F. Wagner lexikon. Cotta. 1883.

GOLTHER, WOLFGANG. Richard Wagner as poet. McClure, Phillips & Co. New York. 1907.

GRIBBLE, G. D. The master works of Richard Wagner. Everett & Co. London. 1913.

GROVE'S Dictionary of music and musicians. Macmillan. New York.

GRUMMANN, PAUL HENRY. The musical dramas of Richard Wagner. University of Nebraska. Lincoln. 1930.

HADOW, SIR WILLIAM HENRY. Richard Wagner. T. Butterworth. London. 1934.

HADOW, SIR WILLIAM HENRY. Studies in modern music. Seeley & Co. London. 1895.

HASSARD, J. R. Richard Wagner at Bayreuth. F. Hart & Co. New York. 1877.

HENDERSON, WILLIAM J. Modern musical drift. Longmans, Green & Co. New York. 1904.

HENDERSON, WILLIAM J. Preludes and studies; musical themes of the day. Longmans, Green & Co. New York. 1901.

HENDERSON, WILLIAM J. Richard Wagner, his life and his dramas. Putnam. New York. 1902.

"The purpose of this book is to supply Wagner lovers with a single work which will fill all their needs. The author has told the story of Wagner's life, explained his artistic aims, surveyed the musical plan of each drama. Not intended to be critical but designed to be expository."

From the Preface.

A scholarly volume written by a competent journalist and music critic.

HIGHT, G. A. Richard Wagner. Arrowsmith. London. 1925.

BIBLIOGRAPHY

HIGHT, G. A. Wagner's attitude to art. Music and Letters. 4:236-45. London. 1923.

HUEFFER, FRANCIS. Richard Wagner and the music of the future. Chapman & Hall. London. 1874.

HUNEKER, J. G. Mezzotints in modern music. Scribner. New York. 1905.

HUNEKER, J. G. Overtones. Scribner. New York. 1912.

HUNEKER, J. G. Unicorns. Scribner. New York. 1917.

HURN, P. D. and W. L. ROOT. The truth about Wagner. Cassell & Co. London. 1930.

JACKSON, J. P. The Bayreuth of Wagner. J. W. Lovell Co. New York. 1891.

JACOBS, ROBERT L. Wagner. J. M. Dent & Sons. London. 1935.

JULLIEN, ADOLPHE. Richard Wagner, his life and works. 2 vols. J. B. Millet Co. Boston. 1892.

KAPP, JULIUS. Richard Wagner (in German). Schuster & Löffler. Berlin. 1910.

KAPP, JULIUS. The women in Wagner's life. Translated by Hannah Waller. A. A. Knopf. New York. 1931.

KOBBÉ, GUSTAV. Wagner's life and works. 2 vols. G. Schirmer. New York. 1896.

KOBBÉ, GUSTAV. Wagner's music dramas analyzed, with the leading motives. G. Schirmer. New York. 1904.

KOHT, HALVDAN. The old Norse Sagas. American-Scandinavian Foundation; W. W. Norton & Co. New York. 1931.

KREHBIEL, H. E. Studies in the Wagnerian drama. Harper. New York. 1904.

LAVIGNAC, ALBERT. The music dramas of Richard Wagner and his festival theatre in Bayreuth. Dodd, Mead & Co. New York. 1902.

LAWRENCE, FREDERIC. Musicians of sorrow and ro-
mance. C. H. Kelly. London. 1913.
LICHTENBERGER, HENRI. Richard Wagner (in German).
C. Reissner. Dresden. 1899.
LIDGEY, CHARLES A. Wagner. E. P. Dutton & Co. New
York. 1899.
LIPPERT, WOLDEMAR. Wagner in exile. G. G. Harrap
& Co. London. 1930.
LORENZ, ALFRED. Das Geheimnis der Form bei Richard
Wagner. Munich. 1924-33. 4 vols.

MAGNÚSSON, EIRÍKR and WILLIAM MORRIS. Voelsunga
Saga: The story of the Volsungs and Niblungs, with
certain songs from the Elder Edda. Walter Scott Pub.
Co. New York. 1870.
MANLY, MARTHA. Bibliography of biographical material
on Richard Wagner, 1900-33. Columbia University.
New York. 1933; Typewritten. New York Public
Library.
MANN, THOMAS. Past masters and other papers. A. A.
Knopf. New York. 1933.
MAUD, CONSTANCE ELIZABETH. Wagner's heroines. E.
Arnold. London. 1896.
MEINCK, DR. ERNST. Die sagenwissenschaftlichen
Grundlagen der Nibelungendichtung Richard Wagner's
(in German). Emil Felber. Berlin. 1892.
MOROLD, MAX. (Pseudonym of Max von Mellenkovich)
Richard Wagner (in German). 2 vols.
MOROLD, MAX. Wagner's Kampf und Sieg (Wagner's
struggle and victory). Amalthea-Verlag. Zürich. 1930.
MUNCKER, FRANZ. Richard Wagner, a sketch of his life
and works. Translated by D. Landman. Buchner.
Bamberg. 1891.

NEUMANN, ANGELO. Personal recollections of Wagner.
Henry Holt & Co. New York. 1908.

BIBLIOGRAPHY

NEWMAN, ERNEST. Fact and fiction about Wagner. Cassell & Co. London. 1931.

NEWMAN, ERNEST. The life of Richard Wagner. A. A. Knopf. New York. vol. 1, 1933; vol. 2, 1937; vol. 3 in preparation.
The most thorough and scholarly biography since Glasenapp. Considered the best biography for up-to-date material. It also includes a survey of the musical, economic and social conditions of Europe, as affecting Wagner's career. (Martha Manly)

NEWMAN, ERNEST. Stories of the great operas. Garden City Pub. Co., Garden City, N.Y. 1928-30.

NEWMAN, ERNEST. A study of Wagner. Putnam. New York. 1899.

NEWMAN, ERNEST. Wagner. Brentano. New York. 1904.

NEWMAN, ERNEST. Wagner as man and artist. J. M. Dent & Sons. London. 1914; A. A. Knopf. New York. 1924.

NIETZSCHE, F. W. The case of Wagner. The twilight of the idols; Nietzsche contra Wagner. Macmillan & Co. New York. 1896.

NOHL, LUDWIG (K. F. L.). Life of Wagner. Translated by G. P. Upton. A. C. McClurg & Co. Chicago. 1889.

POURTALÈS, GUY DE. The mad King. H. Holt & Co. New York. 1928.

POURTALÈS, GUY DE. Richard Wagner; the story of an artist. Harper. New York and London. 1932.

PRAEGER, FERDINAND. Wagner as I knew him. Longmans, Green & Co. New York. 1892.

REISIGER, HANS. Restless star; the youth of Richard Wagner. Century Co. New York and London. 1932.

ROLLAND, ROMAINE. Musicians of today. H. Holt & Co. New York. 1914.

RUNCIMAN, J. F. Richard Wagner, composer of operas. G. Bell & Sons. London. 1913.

184

RUNCIMAN, J. F. Wagner. G. Bell & Sons. London. 1905.

SCHURÉ, EDOUARD. The mystical idea in Wagner. Translated by F. Rothwell. Priory Press. Hampstead, Eng. 1910.

SHAW, GEORGE BERNARD. The perfect Wagnerite. G. Richards. London. 1898.

SONNECK, OSCAR. Essays in music. G. Schirmer. New York. 1916.

STATHAM, HENRY. My thoughts on music and musicians. Chapman & Hall. London. 1892.

STEIGMAN, B. M. The pertinent Wagnerite. T. Steltzer. New York. 1921.

STEIGMAN, B. M. The unconquerable Tristan. Macmillan Co. New York. 1933.

TAPPERT, WILHELM. R. Wagner, sein Leben und seine Werke (in German). Elberfeld. 1883.

TAPPERT, WILHELM. The Wagner Lexikon (in German). E. W. Fritzch. Liepzig. 1877.

THOMAS, THEODORE. Wagner handbook. J. Wilson & Son. Cambridge, Mass. 1884.

TRETBAR, C. F. Analytical reviews. C. F. Tretbar. New York. 1878.

TURNER, W. J. Wagner. Duckworth. London. 1933.

WAGNER, RICHARD. Briefwechsel mit König Ludwig von Bavaria. 4 vols.
These letters deal with the period from King Ludwig's rescue of Wagner in Vienna and Wagner's death. This period includes the completion and production of *The Ring*.

WAGNER, RICHARD. Letters of Richard Wagner. Selected and edited by Wilhelm Altman. Translated by M. M. Bozman. 2 vols.
Covers the composer's entire life. Contains a chronological tabulation of the major events of Wagner's life.

WAGNER, RICHARD. 175 letters to Uhlig, Fischer and Heine. Breitkopf & Härtel. 1888.

WAGNER, RICHARD. 12 letters to Röckel. Breitkopf & Härtel. 1894.

WAGNER, RICHARD. 200 letters to Liszt. Breitkopf & Härtel. 1887.

WAGNER, RICHARD. My life. Authorized English translation. 2 vols. Dodd, Mead & Co. New York. 1911.

WAGNER, RICHARD. Prose works. (Gesammelte Schriften. E. W. Fritzch. Leipzig. 1871-83. 10 vols.) Translated by William Ashton Ellis. 8 vols. Kegan Paul, Trench, Trubner & Co. London. 1892-99. Sämtliche schriften und dichtungen, 6th edition. Breitkopf & Härtel. Leipzig. 1912.

WALLACE, WILLIAM. Liszt, Wagner and the Princess. Kegan Paul, Trench, Trubner & Co. London. 1927.

WALLACE, WILLIAM. Richard Wagner as he lived. Harper. New York and London. 1925.

WARREN, C. H. The men behind the music. G. Routledge & Sons. London. 1931.

WESTON, JESSIE L. The legends of the Wagner drama. D. Nutt. London (1896) 1903.

WILSON, PEARL C. Wagner's dramas and Greek tragedy. Columbia University Press. New York. 1919.

WOLZOGEN, BARON HANS PAUL VON. Guide through Der Ring des Nibelungen.

WOLZOGEN, BARON HANS PAUL VON. Recollections of Wagner.

WOLZOGEN, BARON HANS PAUL VON. Thematischer Leitfaeden. Leipzig. 1882.

WOLZOGEN, BARON HANS PAUL VON. Wagner's spiritual world.

YOUNG, FILSON. The Wagner stories. McClure, Phillips & Co. New York. 1907.

ZDENKO-KRAFT. Crossroad to Bayreuth (in German). Reuss & Itta. Constance.